The Pebble

The Pebble

Old and New Poems

Mairi MacInnes

University of Illinois Press

Urbana and Chicago

Library of Congress Cataloging-in-Publication Data
MacInnes, Mairi.
The pebble: old and new poems / Mairi MacInnes.
p.   cm.
ISBN 0-252-02571-7 (alk. paper)
ISBN 0-252-06794-0 (pbk.: alk. paper)
I. Title
PS3563.C34458 P44 2000
811'.54—dc21   99-050489

1 2 3 4 5 C P 5 4 3 2 1

For Mairi Clare Rodgers McCormick and John George McCormick,
with love and astonishment

Acknowledgments

"I Look for Him Everywhere," "Soft Fruit," "Passion," "Missing," "In Hospital," "Prothalamion," "Ladies' Lunch," "Hard Lives," appeared originally in *The New Yorker,* as did a shorter version of "Why Poetry." All are reprinted here by permission of *The New Yorker.*

"The Scots in America," "Grandfather," "Learning Another Language," "Hardly Anything Bears Watching," "Reading Cavafy in Translation," "Fraud," "Three Cat Poems," "The Present Tense of Machines," and "I Object, Said the Object" are reprinted by permission from *Herring, Oatmeal, Milk & Salt* (Quarterly Review of Literature International Series, XXII, 1981).

"Mass," "Ten in the Morning," "Ten at Night," "Soft Fruit," "The Old Naval Airfield," "Objets d'Art," "Forty Years in a Moorland Parish," "Among the Sea Islands, Georgia," "At Five the Train," "The Bridge at Salamanca," "Nicholas," "Welcome to Mendocino," "The Anarchist," "The Two-Man Saw," "The Fields of Light," "I Look for Him Everywhere," "The Cave-In," and the excerpts from "The House on the Ridge Road" are reprinted by permission from *Elsewhere & Back* (Bloodaxe Books, Newcastle-upon-Tyne, 1993).

"Traveling North," "The Given," "November Digging," "Hard Lives," "Ladies' Lunch," "The Grimshaws," "In Hospital," "Four Kinds of Bird," "The Ghostwriter," "The Rehearsal," "Insight," "The Caul," "Plymouth, 1945," "Passion," "Finn's People," "At the Géricault Exhibition," "Missing," and the poems from the sequence "The Engagement" are reprinted by permission from *The Ghostwriter* (Bloodaxe Books, Newcastle-upon-Tyne, 1999).

Some of these poems and others appeared originally in *The New Republic, The Hudson Review, The Yale Review, Columbia, Sewanee Review, The Tri-quarterly Review, Quarterly Review of Literature, The Nation, The Ontario Review, Threepenny Review, Lines, The Independent, PEN New Poetry I & II, The Observer, New Statesman, Poetry Wales, The Spectator, The Times Literary Supplement, Joe, Stand.*

Contents

From *Splinters* (1953)

Theomachy

Few can do without it. We have grown
from a blank by it. Its fire led us into the land
in time we called our own. Using it as a glass we scanned
busy and cold the world from which we'd come.
Cradling it as a doll we learned how to love and to sing,
although, poor creature, it was blind and deaf and dumb
and made of wood! Not even living!
Oh it was father and mother to whom we returned
weeping. It tongued us in Italian. Its further shore
resounded with tides drawing on rivers of vast Americas.
It figured the lovely one of an early dream.
It was the ash tree that was always in the garden
whose round black arms madonna-like bore heaven
and it was kind as lonely streetlamps are
when there is neither moon nor star.

Laughing at it at last we rejected it and called ourselves free.
But sometimes it can still be discerned.
In the orchestra'd day it may suddenly put its little head on your hand.
I have heard the sound of it pausing on the dark landing
or felt it watching over the heads of the crowd.
And then I am touched with affection and resentment and fear,
but I never go to the door and I never look round.

From *Herring, Oatmeal, Milk & Salt* (1981)

The Scots in America

"The Scots is a proud people,"
said my aunt in Scotland
who had been a great beauty.
"The English is an ignorant people."
Her dark hair had waved to her waist,
and her eyes were as black as a crow,
and she'd four tall brothers
who'd done well in the world.
Often in England I heard the great music
of messages in Gaelic
breaking through the midnight telephone.

"The Scots is a proud people."
Damn it, but I was stupid from my sojourn
in the wrong quarter,
speaking but the one tongue
and that of the ignorant world.
Yet I was acquainted by proxy with
hills, isles, and bottle-green seas,
and hankered reverently after
the wail and strum of the pipes
and the shivering single voices
celebrating love and war, and
my aunt examining my horse face exclaimed,
"Och, Mairi, you're a MacInnes!"

The Scots is a proud people,
so I went proudly to the Highland Service
held once a year among the Presbyterians
of Doylestown, Pennsylvania,
to show where I stood.
But the English is an ignorant people,
and I was surprised to hear the minister,
Mr. Vanderboost, wore borrowed kilts
and the ten pipers in full Highland fig
were costumed by Canadian mail order.
None of them had set foot in Scotland,
and it didn't matter, for when they played
the ancient airs of the Covenanters
as on a sequestered moor, no eye was dry,
and a summer storm whipped up outside
to rip the soft leaves from the churchyard trees
and drench the church's plain glass windows
with an almost familiar rain.

Grandfather

Once he passed eighty, the old man tired.
His milky second wife had tantrums every day
over the nine proud daughters he had sired
upon a long-dead saint; and they,
removed and married from his rich estate,
bothered him daily with a needless stealth
in common love and duty to relate
their petty news and ask about his health.
His thick white hair seemed merely blond as theirs,
they boasted to their friends, his teeth as sound,
his wits as agile as his youngest heirs'.
They said he'd walk for miles his watered ground,
by his word made grassy as an English home,
to order the fruits and flowers he found
the peacock plenty of the southern sun
ripened unflawed, to make life beautiful.

But he could never rest. Nothing was his,
godlike, to enjoy alone. His animal
dimensions demanded the antithesis
of godlike calm. He was his own man still.
He took to driving out beyond the sphere
the women knew, to exercise his will
in unknown businesses. For many a year
they were afraid to ask him where he'd been—
and when at last he died, their fears blazed.
But they were wrong. Each claim had passed his screen

9

and got its due. The patient lawyers raised
no end of land and stock: item his love—
the bright free darlings of his bitter age—
a string of racehorses; beyond, above
possession, things bought in his rage
to stand free and command, or else to flout
his heirs, they thought, as he infirmly gazed
upon them wildly running and his time ran out.

Learning Another Language

In another part of the forest
    the thrushes sing different phrases.
In each part, the melodies are distinct.
    Castaway on the massive body of the world
(sky overhead pale and empty as a page)
    you, poor fool, feel flints puncture your skin.
O self! O drench of meaning!
    But you answer dead as a dead egg.

Mouthing these sounds
    you peel with the heat of the sun.
Blister swells by blister.
    That orb, it is like seeing your lover
stripped of his wrappings,
    turned knobbly, white, garishly sexed
and common as an apple.

Wake from a dream of social consequence
    and find you have a third hand
or two heads or four feet—
    by this monster-maker of contiguity
you get inklings of meaning.
    Disentangle what's your lover and you,
you're back with the razors of existence,
    which wound and wound.

This is not to fly any more
   but go on hands and knees.
This is speaking only a fifth of what you want to
   and the words still speaking otherwise
aiming to break you, as the earth does
   when you horse all over it pretending it's yours.
Adam felt this at his appalling loss.
   The world is big and stubborn and doesn't yield.
Behind you is the angel with the sword.

Hardly Anything Bears Watching

Hardly anything bears watching.
Bricks and stone
have lost their intense surprise.
For years I kept my trust in things.

Even beyond the last parishes
fringed with refuse,
hills drown beneath the surveyor's rod.
They too lie perfectly numb.

The old parabolas of socialism,
spirals of love,
make hope the habitat of the soul.
But hope's not native to the blood.

No comfort from the boy who draws
upon my memory of bombs.
The man recalls
brave days on a far-off sea.

Picture after picture fails.
When I was young
the pavement curbs were made of stone,
a substance like my fingernails.

It is not like that any more.
I do not see
the essential life of inorganic things.
Humanity has covered all.

Reading Cavafy in Translation

He would never have liked me, a woman
who's ample and hopeful and hardworking,
bothered by sentiment, neither stylish nor austere;
yet the loveless cadences of his translation
warm me like an old friend from the capital
met by chance on a provincial street.
His observations are witty and precise;
like good stones in a jeweler's window
they give out fire; they are the bounty of a fortunate life.

I understand too that the original contains
a familiar sadness about the civilization
falling away behind us, and a dry contempt
for our inept love of the present
that flares sometimes, like beacons before Armada.
A clever fellow, he'd be amused to see me mourn
the sky's slow clouding over and my loss of the good to come.

Fraud

Nothing can equal the humdrum fraud
in her eyes, bleary behind glass,
voyeur at balustraded flop,
and fixed on those who pass.
Sure of her corner in the trade
perhaps she pities people on the street,
bankrupts through the world's demands.
What can equal her self-deceit?
She turns in flower-print askance
and soft blind lids half-raises on
that plaza of the double bed.
Satiate with totting up emotion,
she'll let on later to the old cabals
of knitting mothers and restless girls
about the funds her men have raised
on that white square, and how the world's
last expeditions mustered here
to scale those private peaks
or ascend prodigious river—
adventure, to her ravished mind,
grander than some muddy poke
about the unknown earth.

Still, morning after sleep provokes
this glance through sunlit windows.
The sky returns the thrust of things,
which name themselves, demanding action.

She notes the enormous force which clings
to objects isolated.
"Remaindered," she thinks, "they break
of themselves. So lovers who return
find women alien for their sake,
and shorn of honor and the itch,
they think they're parallel aligned,
a pair of wheels that never meet.
Yet with the dampening of the mind,
their powers glide along the track.
Mouth moves to mouth, and hand to hand."

She fidgets, fabrics crackle, hands
loop deceit. Alone, alone, what harm?
Beyond desire, out of sight,
endless petty waves drove her to the wreck—
except those buildings and the busy sky
repudiate her sacrifice—remote, profane—
while silences afflict her always,
bring her now to tears, for steadfastness,
or something she once admired.

Three Cat Poems

i. Age

Poor old cat—she gives me
the tender kiss of antiquity.
She smells like a pensioner
asking a girl to supper,
a fish supper in a back room.
Her teeth like his are rotten,
poor old cat. Still—

she sidles down when the fire is lit
and sniffs the muzzles
of the sleeping dogs
as if they were juveniles.
One whiff of her ancient breath
and they're rigid.
She stretches out on the rug
to coil and uncoil
until she's warm
and then she'll leap to my lap
and stretch her black paw
out to my face and pat it
as if she still smelled
of grass and roses.

ii. Writing at Night

When I switch on the lamp
the old cat comes.
She finds the light bulb warm
and presses up.
Promptly it's dark;
but each long hair
and the white plush beneath
turn into living technique;
and as she warms,
her eyes lift and beam blue
as when headlights hit,
and who can object?
Even her ears
signal a singular line
save only where nicked
by a long-dead rabbit
who never understood
her genius
was otherwise than his,
she so much resembled him in color,
although in nature not,
and so they fought.

But now I must admire
her muzzle wires
and her back's alp
puffed for my shadowy eyes.
O pretty puss! O nonesuch cat!
Whose life compares with yours?
When she retires, overhot,

my tasks, look,
like plain long fields
furrowed with words
black as these lines
appear.

iii. Kin

A stone budges, something out at sea
that comes in on the tide, alive after all.
I'm lying down. A black-rimmed eye
rises to meet mine. Next
she's tapping my nose to see if I'm dead.
Black mask, snub snout, whiskers,
and the moon eyes, faintly opaque.
She holds her breath, listening.
A hum, white spittle on black lips.

Satisfied I'm still alive, she sinks down
to warm her old pads on my neck
and when I look, after all she's a seal
borne up beside me out of the toiling swell
that stares, close up and childishly,
inquisitive as I row by, because she's heard
humans and seals have married before this;
and our lives flow together for a while.

The Present Tense of Machines

My friend Mercedes is neat by nature.
Neat rows of books she has, neat polished furniture.
Her floors are swept and bright.
Her mirror hangs exactly opposite
pots of pink and green and white
poinsettia, banked so the eye will settle
and flit, and yet return to mark a wrinkled petal
that if it fell might all disharmonize.

My friend Mercedes has also
neat cushioned chairs, soft as the devil,
drawn about a sofa table set with a silver tray.
And look, outside, almost outside the oval
of the eye—neat picket fence, neat elm,
neat roofs that cut a satisfactory line,
neat sun to top the composition.

One day a cat came traveling through the grass,
and sensing he was watched, upreared his head.
Mercedes had her camera poised inside the house.
The pattern was dissolving in a dance
of to and fro. Mercedes, if she were quick,
might center everything with one neat click.

At once the firehouse hooter gave a blast—
the cat ran off, the falling sun
engulfed the clean-cut roofs in flame!

At least, Mercedes hoped, she'd caught the cat
before his upraised head and glaring mask
dropped and were gone. The rest was chaos, Mercedes said.

There is too much you cannot ask.
My friend Mercedes is neat by nature.
She absorbs the action any way she can.
There is always much left over.
Her photos please through strength of pattern
Beyond their edges wildness rages.
But even within, there is a hint of hazard—
movement already unpredictably begun,
where patterns form, and gradually fail.

I Object, Said the Object

Out of the habit, I remembered nothing,
    till, like a drunkard beating on the door,
    she shrieked out, "More!" and more
        she had to have.
It was our anniversary. The devil longed
for rings and songs and colored rocks and tinsel.

I wish the police would fix her.
    They'd end her screams with an axe's chop.
    What bliss to hear that yell lopped off!
        Think of the blank
flowering, and then her coiffed acquaintance
relishing her visceral history and sad finis.

I wonder now just how I could have picked her.
    Liable, was she reward? Her loss lobotomy?
    Was she the fundamental shifting at the eye
        of penetrating pain?
Do magical mischances falter without her, the needle
in vision, for earth to pivot on, like an apple?

Whatever she meant once, appreciation's over.
    Today was bad. Tomorrow will be worse.
    Some hormone malady has made her haggish,
        storming the stairs,
mouth agog to the quivering uvula,
taut hands like blown-up gloves waggling disaster—

day after day I send for the doctor,
    and let his hollow needle intercept the kill.
    Thankfully I watch the boggling congeal,
        the blubbering less.
Sobered, she recovers rapidly,
her eyes awash like two great silly puddles.

And then she swears she's never loved me more.
    She takes me in her big caress,
    delicate diva, apt to bless,
        hand on my head,
as if by blubbing we grow richer and closer,
instead of always poorer and more cold.

But soon high-horsed again, she hops away,
    and sorry that I've let her be ridiculous,
    and slow to monkey with the maladress
        that she displays,
I let her bolt and wander, and play herd
upon the unsteady spending of her miscellaneous powers.

So it may happen, one night noble and serene,
    the last phut firework of her endeavor done,
    she'll turn, sane, cool, and say, "Come,
        bring down your sheep.
November's leaning on the fells, and Cassiopeia
leans down to chant her song. Count your last lambs."

Heart-full and grateful then I'll bid them come,
    their mouths like filmstars' ravaged and remote
    uttering sounds unchosen, spontaneous, not
        chidden, flocking,
my lambs, crowding to me, a stranger that says,
"What is it that you want? Is it this? Or this?"

From *Elsewhere & Back* (1993)

Mass

i.

Someone said in a dream, "Flying's dead easy—
just give yourself to the air."
It was true. I tripped on a top stair
and took off like a Frisbee.
Stairs rivered beneath in the hall's arroyo,
sun flashed through windows,
and I saw that the carpet
approached like a rig of flowered silk
or the leaf canopy of a rain forest—
and I caught at a bough or banister
and dropped down unhurt.

Yet unexpectedly the forest
still went past, and how dense,
how weighty and immediate,
the outer world was!
I floated still, I did not exist
minute after minute but in a burst,
all at once, weightless, a rocket
that fired its stars before it fell.

ii.

Last night there was rain
after a summer of drought
and mushrooms cropped in old pasture.
Today I met women gathering them,
a line seen far-off climbing the hill,
their faces touched by the October sun,
strung out, stooped, companionable,
mothers and the mothers of mothers,
neighbors from the nearby village.
I hailed them as a newcomer
out on my own, and they rose up
full height and gazed, gentle as giraffes,
and immediately from crammed baskets
offered me mushrooms . . . weightless
nothing food, food of the dead.
At its moist uncanny touch I felt
the skin on my fingertips to be
no less than the skin of my life,
so heavy and immediate I was,
so dense and full of earth.

Ten in the Morning

The wheatfield's trimmed with poppies, and the drive cuts across it
to where a hall once stood, listed Grade 1, nevertheless demolished
overnight twenty years ago after the contents were sold.
Scaffolding of the old life stands: stable block, servants' house,
barns, cottages, rhododendrons concealing a clotted tench pond,
iron gates to the gardens, iron railings strung with barbed wire
keeping black and white cows in the park under clumped oaks.
The drive resumes the pleasure principle with the prints of horses.
But achieved form and its ethic? Something's been violated.

Now a storm approaches, like a car, head-on. Trees turn to coals
that run with flaming green. The drive is a causeway upon the fire.
The sky crumples and smolders, flashbulbs in the valley.
Now soft summer rain fills eyelashes, now green's doused to ash.
Something's been turned aside. What's shifting things here,
why am I peeved, now the sun's out and I can walk dry the two miles
    home?

Ten at Night

The dog's ear's white
within its flap.
How cold it is,
this summer night!

How loud it was
with tractor and mower
as Ken the farmer
mowed winter grass

with John to follow,
toss and gather,
and cart after cart
despatched to silo

throughout the day
around and around
throughout five fields,
throughout the day.

The last cut in,
the machines chug off.
The day was deaf.
We walk the lane

giddied by hush
in the green-hung air,
by the clarion clear
moon on the edge.

Below my bedroom
the fields stretch out
smoother than linen.
Below walks a woman

not given to smiles,
grandchild in arms,
the farmer's wife.
Whatever she feels

yields to her presence.
The child looks out
from her head height,
his hand on her face.

An ancient shawl
enfolds them both.
She glides likes a boat
upon a canal,

beneath his weight
not shifting him,
not pointing out.
The long day's work
has made him light.

Soft Fruit

Our lanes turn on the ends of fields—
a legacy of medieval
Danish land tenure, I'm told.
Hence the bends are atrocious:
folly to whip past, as two cars did
at midnight last Saturday
doing at least eighty—
two blasts of noise and light,
two spasms, pangs, and gone—

except, just over a humpbacked bridge
on the dark and silent bank
one car, upside down,
wheels softly astir
in a stink of burnt rubber—
and answering to flashlights and voices
two faces in the interior
peering out, with silly smiles:
safe, of course, perfectly intact—

in the dark of the bush
surrounded by frightful thorns
two ripe gooseberries hanging,
luscious, asking to be picked.

The Old Naval Airfield

I looked out Henstridge lately,
somewhere where it always was,
even then, without maps or signs,
and thought of Philip, chief flying instructor,
brave Philip, who soon was dead;
long ago, though, many years ago.

Pretty old, bosky old, footpath
country, and nothing was familiar
till suddenly the dull lane
roused me. A humpbacked bridge
over a disused railway led me
to B Camp that was: now a wood and a shed.
Opposite, the Wessex Grain Company—
storage silos that hummed
in the afternoon air like planes.

On the edge of the field, a bunker gradually
took my eye. A well-turfed barrow?
No, dear God, the rusted roof of a hangar
half-fallen in—and over the field, look,
Philip's control tower, a tall wreck
marooned in breaking waves of grass.

Survival is a form of murder.
My father ran round the garden in the dark
shouting, "She's dead, and I could've

done more for her. I could have, and I didn't."
She'd said earlier, "He couldn't do more,
that man, best man who ever lived."
Truth is, you can always do more.
You have to survive, that too, but it's murder.
He lived on, as you do if you can.

Objets d'Art

Castle Howard's festive old hulk
  lies in open fields like an opera.
  Twenty-seven bays and a dome,
parapet with urns and a baroque
pediment upholding three goddesses, one of them Diana.

Rabble crowds arrive from the town,
  park cars and buy tickets.
  What, tickets to architecture?
To this extravagance? To a prodigious fountain?
They sit on the lichened stone and stare and fidget,

seeing a roof mobbed with statues and urns:
  but something else budges—four
  silhouettes pivot, two urns look odd.
Half a dozen peacocks marooned
up there, implausibly high, six blasts of Tyrian color,

begin to shriek their spoiled terrible cry
  and sail off the roof like plates.
  Worth a gasp—each famous tail
steering like a rudder, each crested tiny
head upping like a joystick: how straight

and competent they glide to the lawn,
  and alight, and bob, and bow, and strut!
  Worth a laugh, worth a clap!

From tenement roofs in the Bronx, a storm
barely over, one hell-hot night, during a power cut,

sailed lids, garbage cans and drums
  into a black and flooded street.
  No one in sight, but maniacal jeering.
Only a lost car, headlights on
and suddenly awash to the doors, on a wrong exit

from the throughway, discovered the performance—
  creatures rebounding and plopping
  to and fro in the water, lopsided,
then swinging together by chance,
a chorus rolled by the backed-up flood, radiantly bobbing.

Forty Years in a Moorland Parish

i.m. Rev. J. C. Atkinson (1814–1900)

Men shot the great spotted woodpecker
oftentimes out of Parson's wood.
What with shooting, the parson writes,
and felling of trees, "the visits to the wood
of those harmless interesting beautiful
birds became strangely like angels'."

Guns also took out of his district
the glorious kingfisher and the barn owl,
the merlin, of course, and the kestrel.
As for the multitude of rooks,
magpies, chaffinches, cuddies, thrushes, robins—
summer saw crowds of them cut down
by the casual husbandman with his shotgun.

The code for anger Parson didn't know.
He often took his own gun to the moors,
and yet put crumbs upon his windowsill
to feed his "starving bird pensioners,"
always wondering, indeed marveling
at the rare and ever rarer woodpecker
that still came like an angel.

Among the Sea Islands, Georgia

A half-completed island, this:
mud and marsh lapse into salt water
on the landward side, while
on the coast facing the open sea,
beaches run clean and straight,
forming the original sand spit,
and the land rises from it
with grassland and woods.
So the track along the spine
is half shell, half soil.
Palm and pine grow side by side,
palmetto lying in between, old
wrecked basket chairs,
and there are stands of venerable
evergreen oak, hung with Spanish moss
like ancient flags in a cathedral.
Woods pare off at the end
to the white quick of sand.
Here skeletons of whole trees
lie beached. Hoofprints, delicate shells,
loop in from the dunes.
A dredging sea. Loons and porpoises
fish, far out. The creek nearby
lies furred, killed off
by spillage from brown tannic pools.

Of all who lived here once
to raise their sugarcane and rice,
no man remains, and little else.
Vanished, the lot—the paddy fields,
great house, huts, wharf,
warehouses, whipping blocks.
Only milestones in woods are left,
pointing to lost plantations,
and the gravestones of "Lotty," "Tib."
How sad, somehow, it is,
this scrupulous lack of consequence!

What if the spring lets fall
its present like a canticle,
and snakes coil warming in the path,
and that painted bunting
like a pentecostal flame
flickers in the bush?
The boatman does not care.
He checks his fine gold watch
and says it's time to go.
A squall is coming. We cannot wait.
Nothing to be done but this.
Nothing matters now.

At Five the Train

At five the train left Hendaye
and trundled inland, across
the foothills of the Pyrenees,
bound for Marseille.

At dusk it drew up somewhere,
earth dark, horizon high,
a greenness in the air,
and stars over the hills.

Half the passengers dismounted,
and doors slammed on crowds.
That's how we knew it was Lourdes,
that and the little fires
carried up under the stars.

We sat in the dark carriage,
broke bread and drank wine,
until we couldn't see
what was flame and what star,
and the train took us off to Marseille
in secret, as before.

On the Bridge at Salamanca

For Priscilla Barnum

At the far end of the bridge and out of sight
there is a tremendous clatter of horses.
Then there is silence. A man shouts.
Another clatter. Strange how they hesitate,
until we hear again that frightful shout.
And now we raise our heads and peer,
the horses surge up, and we scatter,
barreling flesh shoves us against the parapets.
The bridge is old and narrow and very long,
(something the Romans left) and so
we have nowhere to run to, none of us.
We are so many, perfect strangers,
city people, not used to herd animals,
or such bright flesh and huge glassy bosses
of eyes or reckless squashing past.

They are not remotely like painted horses
given to marching on palace walls,
all natural piety and acquiescence.
We are amazed by their acrid smell,
and then by their surge of strength,
and their mysterious seesaw, like rocking horses;
though now we see the horses are hobbled.
A two-foot chain between the forelegs
limits each stride to a hop
or burlesque high-heeled waddle.
And so we smile, how can we not smile—
they look after all quite silly.

The burly herdsman is angry;
he shouts impatiently and waves his stick,
for the crowds impede the passage of his horses.
At the very end of the bridge he waits.
The horses lurch down a bank to their pasture
under high trees by the river,
and lower their heads and start to graze.

Relieved, amused, we look from the parapet.
Beside the horses, under an awning
stretched between bank and pole,
a baby and a girl are fast asleep,
fast fast asleep on mattresses.
The herdsman leaves, first thwacking a tree.
The horses after all are hobbled.
The children are quite safe. "Gypsies,"
someone remarks with satisfaction.
Can it be right, to use the open air
like a bedroom? Is it entirely safe?
The horses hop at random, grazing,
drinking from the river, careless,
spreading out further and further.

Nicholas

Dead Nicholas
smiles out of the photograph
on the stairs of the borrowed house
and I recall that when he was
a boy, put to bed, he'd smiling
stealthily reappear
His steps and voice
are now a man's default

though too he's ever present,
a dislodged marble
dropping daily from stair to stair
past the eternal photograph
of himself once smiling
out through the front door
and into the street

a wrecker's ball
hauled back on its chain
and swung against a building
till the windows pop
and the frames collapse
and remaining walls let go

Welcome to Mendocino

To Helen Wheelwright

I.

A tremendous sea, covered with experienced waves.
Crumbling sandstone cliffs, their rock lodes,
their lofty citadels, cut out and marooned.
Seaweed, sea lions, and a set of pelicans
assumed, and the sea passing them by,
the mastering element, the present controller.

At Mendocino in the last century
the sea looked purely good.
It was what men had to sail on and fish,
and what brought them there in the first place.
The land, too, looked good to mine and sow
and bear crops like other land. Accordingly
men built tall sporty houses in a spacious grid
right on the cove. The grand fronts
they painted pink, green, ocher, blue,
variously lit by the classical Pacific
flashing up the streets' divide.
A stroll through brambles to the shore
brought them a prospect of their neighbor
sea's abundance of color and detail,
which made them smile, so well they understood.
They went home to add a superfluous fret
of wooden filigrees to eaves and rails,
shingles cut and overlapped like scales on fish,

a delicate fanlight with glass over a door,
an outside staircase twined like morning glory.

2.

The wayfarer runs his Honda up One
some ninety miles, half a day from San Francisco,
just to sleep in an old brass bed and eat breakfast

at one of the new inns of famous Mendocino.
The embroidered sheet turned down so bravely O,
the comforter and three lace pillows, their puffed feathers.

The bathtub with brass taps and lion paws.
The frilly white curtains. Old elephant cypresses
outside, flouncing their own black lace.

Soft as the light, womanly warmth up the mahogany stair.
Coffee, and biscuits baking. A pink appliquéd table cloth,
pots of honey and jam, fluted cups, zinnias in a jug.

Silver spoons, knives with bone handles.
China plates wreathed with painted ivy.
The November sun of an old lamp.

Pin thin, the innkeeper in her tight blue jeans
    and her sky-blue T-shirt and running shoes.
        Her body bends in an arc like a tossed net

as she stoops to the sweet-breathing old black oven
    and takes out six bread tins
        filled with her own version of zucchini bread.

◎◎

Down through the grid the tourist, touched with fire.
    Sunlight shoots from the experienced sea.
His eyes prickle. His wallet's heavy.
    He'd live here too if he had the money.
He'd *thrum* with artists in an *atelier,*
    ankle-deep in shavings, and make fine things.
He muses from shop to shop and buys expensively,
    the sea at his back, the malign neglected sea.

◎◎

Outside each shop, baskets of geraniums
bright in their crowd of leaves.
A hard wind from the sea. The flowers freshen.
Pretty red petals lick the sidewalk bricks.
And near the dump and its fallen fence
amaryllis as in Greek Sicily,
fleshy amaryllis all in pink,
pink trumpets with a golden tongue
in fullest voice, amaryllis on the fields of Etna,
belles of the ancient world. "Naked Ladies,"
frowns the prim innkeeper, and slashes off their heads.

3.

Unionised labor's gone inland,
gone to the back country,
where the sea is musing and gentle,
far up a river where the tide turns
among trees and fields and mills.
The only knowledge of the sea now
is a slightly moving, tearing bite,

48

the single symptom of flamboyance.
It's a quiet element for loggers
who float huge trunks in booms
and tether stakes in watery roads
in a basin broad as a town,
and live by the close light of a wood
in houses the color of old fish,
discarded catch chucked out on a shore.

4.

Here come the two Marys in their Toyota.
They've pawed through the merchandise. They're angry.
The stuff's meant for someone with more money.

The shopkeepers, though, wear a nuptial look.
"Goodness, how I love my mother," their young man's
little smiles say, as they hover over

a priceless trinket no Mary wanted in her young days
but would be glad of now. But Mary has Mary,
half blind though the one is and the other wheezes.

So what's the sea been up to?—clambering
through briars and paper wrappers down to the cove
where the sea's whimpering, spilling and mowing.

Its quake-strewn ramparts of hewn stone
meet expectations as always and as the Marys do,
since the sea is without necessity,

two-thirds of the earth's surface
but unmarketable, unconserved, not taken into account,
even its fine storms improperly assessed, often,

and, unpredicted, called calamities,
as if that nailed them. The sea, admired,
now becomes admirable, and gratis to the point of tears,

like the moose that wandered past the back door once,
in Maine, two calves at heel as big as trucks,
the three of them sauntering into a Mary's life

as if they were safe there for good.
What if the beach tilts against one's eyeball,
coming down, black visor over white metal,

and the other's breath is pelted with grit
until she gasps? The magnificent unplaced desire
at liberty here soon has the Marys amused.

The sea becomes their spokesman, mouthing its vowels
between their toes and shoulder-high out there,
it pushes its roars and chirrups into their ears,

it slides wet and heavy into their hands.
And its floor—not like a kitchen floor's
aberration in dirt and stains, but single,

whole. Its stones, now, ovoid and heavy,
that the sea has rolled in the river mouth,
even dried, smell faintly of its breath.

The Marys forage for some that are perfectly round.
They're at home here, with their old measure,
the packaging peeled from the rest of the world.

5.

Chaperones with huge beach towels
held out for naked bathers:
in the cool of the garden where the stones will go,
the lords of language with their nets.
Globed silences, placed exactly,
with many a considerate cocking of the head
and standing back to judge the effects.
Bougainvillea, jasmine, ivy, myrtle,
and other jabberers with colored hats
advance with their paraphernalia of roots
as the garden sways at its anchor,
the perfectly round stones of Mendocino
brought back by the two Marys.

6.

The sea grumbles far away, the sea devoid of honor,
gobbling, dangerous, cold, forever
missing something, it doesn't know what.
"Oh, for God's sake!" it cries, and bellows all night
through the lace curtains of the famous Mendocino inn.
What if the only thing wrong is the moon?
The sea wants its words too, to declare that
it is various and detailed and craves to be looked at,
and gives of itself for ever. It only imagines it is hungry,
full as it must be with continent wolfed.

The Anarchist

Fénéon passed out most of his pay
to the needy before he reached home.
The rest kept his mother. He married out of pity
a friend whom divorce had compromised,

but maintained his old mistress
and fathered on others two bastard sons.
Bon bourgeois, functionary in the War Office,
but wild for art, he saw the *Illuminations*

of Rimbaud into print and the last verse
of Laforgue; explained Seurat, defended Signac,
hailed Van Gogh. But as critic his chief act
was as an anarchist, reverse

logician, planting a bomb in a crowded café—
a flowerpot bomb, fuse in a hyacinth.
When it went off, a painter lost an eye.
At the trial, Fénéon, impassive as a sphinx,

was acquitted, thanks to innocent friends.
His ironies stayed secret and immune
over the next fifty years, their ends
unimportant, and the self hard as a stone
jiggled in a pocket, kept decently in hand.

The Two-Man Saw

"You are cutting down a tree!"
Sagacious, in fresh cotton,
she advanced among the furious geese
to the edge of the lawn and the bald old elm
we were at work on.

"Do you know how to cut down a tree?"
We paused while she readied advice,
and over the clangor of geese
nodded as gay as we could, once more
a colonial couple in the wilderness,

and bent to the great Victorian saw,
one on each handle, rowing the huge
blade between us, one to the other,
as she watched, and the geese
extended their black nibs and hissed.

We were coated in sweat, you and I,
floured with sawdust, our eyes
starting and streaming with heat,
but how could we miss the sweet sap smell
that rose from the saw's stroke,

as of a saint's blood, fragrant, incorruptible,
or not feel the elm's veer on its ropes
while, powered with regret, we sawed like maniacs,

and the saw bound, and came free,
and bound? And the instant before the elm

yielded and swayed down to the ground,
boughs a-crack, an unknown miraculous
power became manifest among us,
as if a hero had died
in an epic, in front of his white-faced enemies.

The Fields of Light

Again and again, a presence in the clearing
    that was the clearing itself;
the row of firs in snowy quilts,
    the parting of sky and snow.
Again and again the cold unpainted room,
    the dead fire, the tap's needle of cold,
the cooling skins of the bed, the kettle's fuss,
    the bang and commotion of the furnace.
Twigs kindled, waggling fingers of warmth.
    The days began by writing themselves.
Dark words ploughed the fields of light.

In the afternoons, in the riding barn,
    old William waited; twenty years old,
plump in his baize winter coat,
    ancient and patient and horse. Round and
round the riding barn among the competent
    petulant well-mounted little girls
thumped William, reliable Pegasus
    for the reliable winter poet.
Later, blown, the unsaddled William
    examined his stall, munched hay, propped a hoof.
He may have remembered Homeric gallops,
    leaps, falls, great treks home in rain
after getting lost, long miles from home;
    or that was the poet, steering a metal vehicle
back to the rented cabin in the woods.

On the very last day, the firs written up,
        the snow, the fire, the light and dark,
and William, all caught and bound,
        the poet drove out of the clearing in the trees
to where the route for the city
        zippered up the divided woods,
the fields of snow, the icy marshes,
        the great lovely vistas opened down valleys.

But a mile or two out, there was William
        entering the highway from a country lane
at full gallop, riderless, tail high as a flag,
        two silly colts along, a band of marauders
drunk with merriment, that sent the traffic
        braking, parking, flashing hazard lights
while elementary horseplay went on—
        such bucking and cavorting, squeals and nips!
A poet could scarcely believe it.

Then, rapture spent, William permitted a running girl
        to catch up, and submitted to a halter
and so walked home to the barn, the colts
        trotting obediently to heel—but not before
he had let out a neigh like a clarion
        and produced a prodigious buck, to show
the drivers edging into the flow of traffic
        how unreliable he was, how original,
how easily he broke the dark lines
        the poet had laid over the fields of light.

I Look for Him Everywhere

For John

Walking over the bridge early—
the level of the lake still sunk
    in darkness, and the pale road
barely lifted out of the murk—
    I found a man established
already at the parapet,
    arms out, fingers splayed,
facing sunrise and a bank of trees
    drab from last week's heat.
He refused to turn at my footfall.
    I trotted past him like a sheep,
resenting him. It was hardship
    to be sacrificed to his piety,
the penance in his ritual,
    whatever it was. And instead of dawn,
solitude, and the lake scanned
    for clarity as it reached the sky,
to have this lumber I'd no use for,
    cramming a space meant to be bare!—
I still carry him, arms out, in my mind.

Last month, in Yorkshire, I hunted down
Charles Waterton's Walton Hall,
    pillared and porticoed stone box,
brown paper color, on its lake.
    Brick houses now look down on it

from the Wakefield side. On the other hill,
    a man ploughed up a great pale square
that darkened as I watched,
    and I recalled how Waterton
at the end of 1824
    came back here from the Amazon
clad in top hat and old frock coat—
    the pockets ideal for specimens
he was then to label and display
    in glass cases, for visitors.
He made a sanctuary for birds
    out of the Walton woods and lake.
I've read of him, in later years
    he'd only to open his front door
and to extend his arms
    and they converged from every cover
greedy to be fed: bevies at his feet,
    wings on his chest, angel on hat,
two shoulders feathered thick,
    and two arms' worth of birds.
Nothing's left but house and birds—
    widgeon, mallard, teal and coot,
pochard, Canada goose—maneuvering
    everywhere upon the moat.
His singular gesture folds to rest,
    a butterfly shut in a book.

    Now you're swimming in our pool.
Five laps of the same measure,
    surging with uniform stroke,
and you are limber, you emerge.
    The water streams off your grizzled beard

and chest and thighs. You move with towel
    to the luminous shade of the grape arbor,
a man getting on for seventy,
    thinking of this and that, who chuffs
as he rubs the great colored cloth
    over the verdigris of his flesh.
Out in the sun the water heaves
    in a glittering groping for what's gone.
Did it know what it had as I know it?—
    That nakedness, that transfusion of life?
How easily now belief arrives,
    and worshipfully claims nothing!

The Cave-In

What did he say, that blinded dusty boy,
when he was dug out?
                —That first the darkness
of the cave-in lay identical outside and in,
across his eyelids; that the cries
he shrilled met stone and cried back to him
as echoes. He was imprisoned by an entire hill.
So humble and colossal it was, he cried until
the cold stationed in his boots wormed up
to his armpits, and threaded itself on vertebrae
and folded round his belly in a web.
So his tears dried up in convulsive shivers;
the taste of salt and tannin dried out his head.

When he came to, he heard thumps—
his heart, perhaps, or a pavement tamper,
and increasingly nearer, a flutter of water,
a streaming, pounding, a clatter of hoofs
that halted almost on top of him. He knew the advance
of a heavy animal, he smelled sweet grass
on its breath, and acrid hairiness of hide,
before he felt on his ears the bloom
of huge warm lips, tenderly, curiously applied,
and the nudge of damp nostrils on his neck,
and recognized the pushiness of a great beast
used to its own success.
                    He got up (he said)

oh, joyfully, and touched the warm and rounded moleskin
surrounding tons of brilliant flesh,
and felt it glide under his hands, and twitch, ticklish,
till in a gigantic snatch it bolted off
slap into the rock, and there the skull and skeleton
sparked like a lode, or luminous fossil,
the bones of a horse running; while he heard,
a good way off, the noise of hoofs.
What a horse was doing there, what it meant,
he'd no time to wonder before the rescuers
broke through the rockfall and found him.

From "The House on the Ridge Road"
An Imaginary History

i. Midwinter, New Jersey

Snow flies through the ribs of the barn
caught like an elk in its thicket
till nothing remains but bone

snow out to inhabit
its delicate derelict house
tipped into a dark wood
lidding the cold chimney
blanking the door   blinding the window
wadding the carriage lane
humping box hedge and rosebush
letting a single white line
unroll between wood and torpid grey light
where cars pass

snow out to penetrate
that broken space where the orchard survives
in front   on crutches
where apple trees are elbow deep
on white tussocks stitched with straw

The long white corridor of the ridge road
flicks past as quick as a marble
The empty house bobs quietly away

leaning into the snow of the rear mirror
a woman in white waving and running
then stopping and looking after me

ii. What They Say Happens

The mother of us all is queening it there.
She is forever sweeping the floor.
A fire of apple logs is burning:

logs of pearmain, russet, pippin—
they blaze on the hearth and puff apple breath
at a row of huddled children.

Their hands are warming like small cold stars.
The mustiness from closed windows and doors
has vanished up the chimney.

The snow windows are full of the snow field
and coils of apple smoke unwrapping over it
and over the road where a woman wantonly stares.

The winter wind snaps smoke out like a sheet.
Strips melt into the dark of the woods,
bending the light, spreading the smell of apples.

The house creaks inside, opening like a wooden flower.
The narrow staircase shudders with delight
as our mother throws the bones
of yet another apple tree upon the fire.

iv. A Desire

Warming in large pale hands:
the blossom of small cold feet.

Tightshut child eyes, heldbreath kiss:
russet apple flesh bite.

Child whispers:
dry apple leaves shifting on grit.

Child weight on lap:
a man's great fruit.

v. The Settlement

But not yet. First a gash in the scalp of the land,
its gold brown hair ripped back,
maple trunks piled and picked clean.
The discarded roots, the burning stocks.
Extracted roots and their sockets.
The lurching of men, the lurching of yoked oxen.
The fires, the smoke, the trampling, the mud.
The cries of men, the creaking of harness.
The smell of new-cut seasoned timber.
The burr of the saw, the chut of the adze.

From the town below, smoke perceived on the ridge.

Later, the great stones forming cellar walls,
enclosing a space instead of occupying it,
and the floor laid over the cellar space,

64

so the house begins to rest on the bottom of its word
and to rise gradually out of it,
darkening the word, estranging it, becoming wooden,
hollow, the hollow heart of a tree.

viii. *The Groundhog*

Dark: a grinding and gnawing.
Leprous buildings coming alight.
Stink of blood.
Click of the ready: ratchet of the clock,
scurry and plink of a blind going up.

On the grass by the barn, a working, a lump:
rawhead and bloodybones.
And, when the gun went off, pandemonium.

Something hurried to the wall
dragging its heavy furs.
Out of a door at a run, thick with desire
for its ancient barbarous flesh,
its huge teeth, its stupidity,
the man caught it, clubbed it till limp,
humped it to the wall
and dumped it over. Back in the kitchen
the house dog nosed his hand.
The children pointed: "Blood! blood!"
as he took off his boots. Fear,
fear and laughter made them choke.

As they wheezed and screamed, he felt again
tremors in his fingertips where the dog's tongue worked,

perceived beast sighs in their small pink mouths,
hatred in their wrong hysteria.

x. Lament for the Children

Where are they off to
so early, the moment it's light?
Where are they off to?
Their kidding and laughter
last night filled the orchard
like tumultuous water
chuckling and splashing
under the keel of a ship.

Where are they off to
in their best? It isn't Sunday—
where are they off to
in their floating white dresses
and serious suits,
young men and women,
flower of the orchard
cut from a hundred boughs?

Where are they off to?
The ridge road is empty.
Where are they off to?
They've gone to fetch winter,
its frosts and gale winds,
to put out the fires
and wrench open windows
and let snow drift on the stair.

xi. A Retreat

The weekly garbage truck
pants up the hill
trailing a smell of midden
Two men
hang on its shoulders
They discharge themselves
up driveways
over snowy lawns
Staggering they return
hefting colored bins
They fire them
into the bunker
of the moaning truck

Freak messages of rot

xii. How It May End

The man's end might be cleaner cut than hers,
a name speaking up out of survey or tax record,
his marginalia in a shelf of books, his look
cropping up in a dozen descendants' faces,
a path he trod through a wood
that never made it into highway
or was quite overgrown,
and a rapt place on a street
where on a summer night he was caught by an air
played in a single bright room of a neighboring house
with a woman at the piano and a boy on a flute;
he saw and heard, and was taken up through the dark

in pleasure; so much so his wife thought
afterward how much she'd missed,
as if he hadn't already embodied her regret,
on her lips a recollected touch,
a bit rough like a Russet,
a bit smooth like a Red Delicious.

She called her neighbors rootless, though,
creatures of a mimic life,
they were so plainly out to laugh
as they swerved to avoid her,
stalwart on the crown of the old ridge lane,
booted like a seaman, cuffed with gray socks,
skirt and cardigan hitched with a pin,
eyes intent under the ancient tam,
her senses seized in the house,
like paper at exit from a door, cut off.
Birds migrated through her mind
and she barely noticed—didn't have to,
her own end never anywhere in sight.
She lay down in traffic now and then
to call attention to the rotten state of the world.
She muttered through town meetings—they knew her well.
When her gaze swivelled at last, she knew
they'd driven past with their understanding,
giggling in their secret heart—
down with relief into driveways
tight between boulder and boulder,
shouldering thinned out trees, nursers of a view.
There they thought of her as answer
to questions that wouldn't come up.
Babies had been born in her bed, hadn't they?

There too the dead had lain, immensely admired.

The neighbors were frivolous, however,
preoccupied with infinity,
clean floors and diamond ceilings.
Whatever she embodied they laid aside
like a photograph or tea-cloth freshly ironed
for the last time.

xiii. A Memory of the Other Country

Still on the snow lane
packed by its tire prints,
she thought of the journey home
over the hills by train

after staying with Margaret
when she was ten—
clear-shot fields, tops white as lint,
bottoms of ash and oak

hammered with snow strokes,
a durable script;
no sound but the engine;
alone in her carriage,

lonely, nothing to read,
only now and then at a halt
the cheerful guard
inquiring how she was,

until the train slid
into her station, a vast sleeve
of gauzy glare and steam
in which her father waited.

When they drove home
through flash of bike
and tram and car and rig
that edged through a sparkling dark,

she told how Margaret
had a delightful family
in the house beyond the hills
surrounded by its woods and fields;

some days they'd sledded
and spent some with ponies afield;
they made up wild games each night
and whispered tales in bed.

At last the train, good little flunky,
ran her home over the fells.
And now she saw herself
a pair of traveling eyes

observing a piecemeal land
finally one; beyond reach,
so much itself she ached;
because she couldn't join it, sad.

And she went quiet for lack of words.
She looked inward

and felt the train still moving
and saw the fell again and heard
murmuring within her skull
Stone, hill, snow, girl.

xiv. A View in Winter

One day soon after I returned
the elm on the ridge went down
snow-clotted till it tumbled,
a dish of dark roots in the air.
The mare rolled in the field
just so last summer, flaunting
her dark rose-spackled belly,
kicking her dark legs until
she staggered up and veered
over the orchard wall, to gorge
on apples, her just reward.

After the fall the elm groans
deep in itself, relieved of its own weight
as it settles, cracking and creaking,
moving into itself, into its heart
until it's at ease this once
with the muffling vast unsurpassable snow.

From *The Ghostwriter* (1999)

Traveling North

The hills step forward.
I am nearly home
at residue: desperate, derelict;
what lies on its back
in the thick of the wood
between two billows of field;
what hides and sulks, the dud, the fool,
indifferent to rescue.

Now it's running for dear life
with its chimneys alive and dead
and mess of roses and the clematis
crawling all over the roof.
What a sight! It is pitiful!
If I catch it I'll give it what for,
and I bet it is filthy,
I bet it can hardly see out,
I bet it is cold and damp,
I bet I'll arrive too late
and it'll just be quiet, big-eyed, shrunk.

Here is order, here in passage.
I take a fix on outlying farms'
single brightnesses.
A thousand sheep glimmer along the bank,

all meant, all bargained for.
I storm up in third gear
and look back on a plain
so vast it must contain everything.
Woods, fields, smoke, haze stretch
its pattern to the cathedral towers
and the two power stations'
five cooling towers each,
twenty miles away,
arguments from the silence
under my hissing tires
repeated again and again as though
I do not take them in.

Another ridge, and I plummet down
between high field edges
in ever tighter curves, to a bend
where the odor of muck
sticks, like a sleeping pig,
and there my windows shine
out of their stone and oak
beyond the beech-tree and the garden,
beyond the garth, beyond the farmer's
last retaining hedge, beyond this business.

It's deathly still in the yard.
Someone is shrinking into the dark
like a fool biting its thumb,
and someone already there,
daemon, or boss, or child
grown tall and critical,

is waiting to put me straight.
The fire will indeed be trim.
Can't I hear the furnace roar?
The beds will be white as brides,
new bread will be hardening,
the sloes disperse in gin
their bluish pungent smoke,
July's hard pickled plums
soften to apricot . . .

Yes, then, I'm wrong.
Oh, I've been wrong,
oh, far too frequently,
made stupid mistakes, got drunk,
become unmanageable; gone off
without compunction.
What is the difference?—I'm back.

The house is waiting, a golden woman.
Her arms are folded, she wears
her contemptuous filial grin.
I'll get out the luggage, go in.
Dear house, I love you best.
Receive me ever kindly as you do now.

The Given

Asthmatic heaven, psychic repletion, air—
the longed-for regimen he long prescribed:
it's here they would have come to spend the day,
in runs and rises where the moors cut loose.
Ecstatic, silent, he'd turn off motor roads
and jolt the Swift down tracks, inch it along
until it stalled. In the end, an ear
to curlews' cries, the whistles grouse invent.
Then, dickey open, he'd get the picnic out.
She'd settle rugs and plates and cups, ignite
the Primus, make the tea. Not what she chose—
lifelong, not what she had in mind. And yet
the warmth of peat and air undid them both.
Below, the old town smoked, the type of hell.

They'd be surprised we too fell in the lap
of hills so casual. Not that we chose
the train to Montreal, the Polish ship,
icebergs off Labrador, the fishing fleets
at ease, the transatlantic haul and thud,
the docks at Tilbury. She'd at least have frowned.
Not what she had in mind. Not what we chose,
either. True, untrue: the toy suburban life
counter and cold. What had it taught us? Flight?
Not what she meant, or he. Things' old shapes
get on with their ancient names, embodiments
of meaning lost, as we ourselves are lost.

The smells of burning wood trash coalesce,
the house of stone comes sailing out of its woods.
A step to the north, moors position themselves;
the skies inaugurate clouds, and winds begin;
the raw ploughed field flickers with rooks and gulls.

November Digging

I am cutting the clearing free from its roots
    Garden will float
free from the adventitious
    the glistening goutweed suckers
ganglias that sprout nettles,
ivy's furred hawsers
the fibrillations of bramble

Sweet light tents me as I fork
    yet what mote flits
into the corner of my eye and out
    hides and reappears and hides
a small brown knowing bird
    drawn to an exposé of flies
three sharp notes
    but there again he hides

When the black crumb's clear
    I'll plant bushes
gooseberry blackcurrant raspberry
    and one day cheat him of their fruit
punnits of soft
    emerald onyx ruby
for all the pies of summer

But in the interim I fork up
    knobs of clenched bulbs

snowdrop garlic aconite
  and china in blue and white
chipped lusterware and *famille rose*
  crude pottery with painted bands
a flint sharp as a knife
  a horseshoe oxshoe hinge key bottle
five four-inch nails handmade
  the upper of a boot
who lives down there to need such things

Would he hear if I sang out
  and push up through the soil
his two white hands to clasp my neck
  and show his white face for a kiss
a kiss that would taste of raspberries

Hard Lives

It was foggy and frosty, not a night to be out,
    and there was no one in the village street,
and nothing moved ahead on the lane
    that led between Stocking Farm and larch plantation.
Grass on the verges stared like the fur of some arctic animal;
    the fog came up like a wall at eye level
and sagged around us like curtains.
    We drove right through it. After all it was easy,
this getting home in winter, we could give lessons

    up to the second when roe deer shot over the headlight tunnel
in the arc of the wipers: left to right funneled
    leaping gray creatures with delicate wet black
eyes and muzzles—and we cried out in shock,
    that thinned into pleasure because they were free of
the world, and their lives were apart, and their exit as soft
    as bolt after bolt of silk tossed to the floor
of the wood and unraveled. The way ahead was wretchedly bare,
    potholed macadam going uphill between fences.

We'd stopped with a jolt. As we restarted, as
    I shifted the gears one by one, as we lost
the fog, climbing, we saw the measure of frost
    stretched over the open field,
the empty barren January field
    (but we'd be home before we questioned anything).

Red eyes in the headlights, shiftings, pale flickerings—
    those were just sheep: solid wool bodies, imbecile faces,
mouths crammed with hay (plenty more hay strewn on the grass).

    It was only days later it hit me how false
perception had been and how misery, what else?
    drew the roe deer from the wood: so famished
they'd fed with the farmer's sheep, so vulnerable they fled
    at the crunch of the car; and more, the world we despised
was open for them to take refuge in
    as it wasn't for us, who weren't secretive, or starving.

Ladies' Lunch

He pocketed one hand and waved the other.
Then I was gone, I suppose, and he went back to that earthy
apartness I fancy he preferred,

and painted, chopped, or scrubbed, and put a record on,
the splendid luminous vacancy of afternoon
fleshed out by the rehearsed emotion

of opera stars whose rival voices
warbled in turn of loves and sadnesses,
regrets, mistakes, and agonies

he might have had to grin at, if I'd been there.
Meanwhile, transfixed in a thunderous hotel bar
I had to read minds like a fortune-teller,

as the bar lacked air and the ceiling pressed down
and bedlam
reigned from the first glass of gin.

I had to touch these other lives, as a child
presses its lips
to the mirror and kisses its very self—

those lizardly eyes, the skin of those cheeks hung loose,
crosshatched mouths; reticulated necks,
heads bobbing yes, yes;

also their hands' mottle, plus an occasional diamond,
dentists' teeth, laughing; the matched teeth of friends—
a creature forty times sliced end to end

to make tissue sections so neatly successful.
I thought of us wandering the world until
we met at this moment, radiantly whole—
and saw with relief how we kicked at reunion
as each woman turned, with her own smile of welcome,
and the worm wriggled in me, the sly hermaphrodite worm.

The Grimshaws

We love other people's lives:
    we need their focus. Take Grimshaw—
the Mr. Grimshaw who killed his wife
    and with a hammer,
pursuing her round the table till she fell,
    when he put her in the outhouse together
with two of her severed fingers.
    No one in the next cottage recognized
so much as a thump.
    The postman saw nothing,
nor the man from the gas board
    who came to read the meter:
he was turned from the door
    with a footling excuse.
Even the traveling hairdresser
    thought she had the wrong day.

Nobody at the shop perceived
    Mr. Grimshaw wasn't the same
as ever, a tidy old incomer,
    deaf but polite (the rare times he spoke),
buttoned up in his camelhair coat.
    The three mornings after the event
when he picked up his newspaper
    were the same as other mornings.
Only the dog frenzied at the window
    alerted the policeman to peer in later

and see Mr. Grimshaw dead on the sofa
 and the blood that spattered the ceiling,
the puddles of blood on the floor,
 the wads of human hair.
The postmaster told a reporter:
 "They were nice people." He meant,
the Grimshaws were like us.
 When they fell off the shelf and were smashed,
we focused on how we were left,
 lopsided and blind, out of money,
instantly recognizable.

In Hospital

I'm an old fool in the guise
of a trusting old fool
and I lie here at one
with a host of other women
somewhere between what we are
and what we think we are

and I think I hear the waves
hurrying inshore one after the other,
fetch of a thousand
thousand waves of generation
and wonder what are the rules
when motherhood's played out
in this world that's a limited whole
and its sides contract
to a women's ward in the hospital

Someone still young
cries in her husband's arms
She came here in the night
I think they've lost their baby,
the woman in her coarse cotton shift
open down the back like a split husk
and the man fully clothed and buttoned and shod
Orpheus who'll return to the light, Eurydice
bound to go under the night with the dead unborn

Better look at the north sky
and the row of terrace houses
on the far side of the railway line
where the Scarborough train slips past hourly,
two silver carriages with a blue stripe
And here is a cheerful monitoring voice
announcing a menu for lunch
(the nurses have been up for hours,
running like flightless birds
in little flat shoes and cockatoo caps)

And now the surgeon reappears
in a graceful palais glide
debonair   a little smile   a nice conspiracy
He sits on each bed and explains
he's transferring his power to us
Who knew the future could be so clear?
Now someone is turning us over one by one
with the dispassionate hand of a beachcomber
Someone will trim us to the bare root.
Oh why can't I rejoice at being taken up?

Four Kinds of Bird

i. The Dunnock

As I lay dreaming on the grass
a dunnock flew up to my face,

and fluttered her wings at my eyelashes,
and presented her pip of an eye at my nose

and looked into my pupil
as if she stood on a windowsill

and made of the intervening glass
a mirror of herself, with lawn and bushes,

and the straggling roses and yew hedge,
and the chair under the apple tree, and the ha-ha ditch

rife with rhubarb and brambles.
Or it was the Eden of my skull

she peered into, with a bird
as plain and brown as herself observed

rustling and shifting. My interior
breathed roses and apples. I had her. No escape.
When she took off skywards, the landscape
was bone hard. A petal stuck on the air.

ii. *The Dipper*

On the bank of the Wharfe,
    a shock of disbelief—
there, there, under the flowing water
    a bird on the river bed!—
she peered among stones
    and gobbled a grub,
a grub or a water beetle.
    How did she learn to hunt like that,
out of her element,
    holding her breath and
taking the prey by surprise?—
    A small bird with sharp eyes
and untypical behavior:
    should I regard her as omen,
or gift, or model?

Just as I bent closer
    simply to admire,
she flew into the air
    in a burst of water.

iii. The Swallow

North of San Diego
    surfer dudes ride the waves
in wetsuits so brilliant
    the colors identify them way out at sea.
Their girls line the beachfront,
    swallows on a wire, twittering and balancing,
in days before the winter migration.

The police have a checkpoint two miles north
    for Mexican immigrants without work permits.
Whole families travel for work to Los Angeles
    crammed in the hidden compartments of a truck.
Dogs sniff them out. Sometimes the *sin documentos*
    run across the highway to hide in the desert.
Signs of a fleeing woman and child
    warn drivers to watch out for these figures,
since many have been killed.

iv. The Cock Pheasant

The reddest of redheads, hung with gold—
ruby earrings, necklace of jet—
cloak of emerald, speckled shirt—
he bursts from the hedge
like a sneeze from the throat.

Mayday, mayday! Universal alert!

The dog alas hangs by a wing.
Oh, Louis Seize, he would escape
the dog, the hand, the guillotine!
Oh, narrow beak and stiff pink tongue,
an arrowhead stuck in the throat!
Oh, black spot of an eye, a pearl!

His corpse afire, I dowse in leaves.
It goes on flaring underneath.
Oh, Louis Seize, on my return
I'll bring you to a kingly feast!

The Ghostwriter

I came to hate the telephone.
I'd leave and make tea and unmissed return

while my subject banged on about love
and her beauty when young—I'd never believe

how she ached when she saw it going!
And there were the husbands and her other men

to be dealt with, and her stage career,
her talent instantly hailed, notices to swoon for,

the command performance in great palaces, et cetera—
Istanbul at her feet, the Middle East, America.

She had our title ready: *Baghdad to Beloit.*
"And so," I interrupted, "is that it?"
and heard her sigh "So . . o . . o . . Darling, can we meet?"

At her elbow I'd sensed the dustiest provinces,
the seediness of Anatolia, the indifference

of midwestern downtowns; aged Emma Bovary
looking for dues the world would pay

"when our book hits the bestseller list."
Who said I'd collaborate? I began to protest,

but saw she was braver than I'd admit,
and something rang sweetly in her self-delight.

So I told her sternly she should understand
to write the book I must have a free hand:

the woman must be silent and the image speak.
That image, unlike her, would hold back;

it would be amused, ironic, sensitive,
to tell of a secret self and an inner life

such as her story called for, to give it worth.
"What *inner life*?" she cried, remembering her youth,
when the sole value was herself.

In the end she went along, suspicious,
repeating now and then we both were ladies,

as if only a lady would respect her soul,
not lift her life as raw material.

I pointed out the voice was hers,
charged with her marvelous marvelous

charm. Look too, I said, what else I'd given her:
insight, logic, clarity, a biting humor.

At first she felt total joy. And then unease—
obscurely put out, unfocused, travestied.

In six months she exploded: "This is your book, not mine.
You've made it up. And lots of it is wrong—

not people, or events, or history—
they're fair enough—but me—the heroine isn't me.

I recognize *you*—quite colorless—plain dull:
my life's been rich and gorgeous and beautiful—

I've paid you plenty. What d'you mean, I can edit?
Get it into your little head, it won't fit
me, your sad book. My God, it's quite pathetic"

I returned manuscripts, tapes, transcriptions.
She struggled alone with her own soft fictions

for half a year, couldn't find anyone else
to work for her, and so gave up. Unfinished,

unappreciated, woman and image eyed
each other with distaste over the ink divide.

A pity: she was so elegant, that image! She
would never have owed me money, or thrown my work away.

And nothing left me but wooden spoons, a pair
the woman gave me, carved from one block. I think of her

when I use them in the kitchen every day,
a craftsman's spoons from Konya, in her own country,

with twelve coats of varnish, smooth as porcelain,
the wood clear beneath in color and grain,
yet harder than wood ever was, as hard as bone.

The Rehearsal

Quiet gathers
   thick as lint
      among the hard chairs.

Summer stands in the street.
   The bare room is
      open and opaque.

The audience crams in
   anonymous, dense,
      then the quartet, slim and quick.

First notes are unclenched,
   They flutter and fan
      and abruptly cut.

A nod, kick start:
   bellies and arms work, piston and crank,
      four crescendos roaring into shallows

climbing a high bank, grabbing or in air,
   stones flying, the quiet
      run through like a village;

and sweating moleskin withers
   and trembling vibrating
      metal handlebars

and body stepping out of its clothes
    and viewing itelf and quite unafraid
        "I am here," it says,

"I am here. You have forgotten,
    haven't you? Don't be afraid,
        you will remember now."

Insight

For Mairi

We plunged down from the summit
  over the slither of scree
till the path jackknifed
  over clints round a baldish moor
and cloughs set in its side
  and welded fields, a hundred of them,
with thorns embedded, and into iron
  woods, faintly aromatic, on a precipice,
harbored in boulders taller than Stonehenge

  till trembling like racehorses
reined back at the starting gate,
  our knees locked, and were agonies,
brakes seized, as stones
  bounded downhill ahead and we stayed,
upright, controlled: we saw
  behind an optic watering screen
the wood, the lake, perfectly black,
  the railway crossing where the train
twice a day gives its excited yelp,
  then the quite invisible house,
roof first (with turrets perhaps),
  and gate ajar, heads swiveling on sticks
from the balconies as we walked in
  wondering what child would dance out then
to meet us—would we know whose,
  the one we had in mind being yet unborn,

her face appearing only in the night,
      her teeth like seed pearls, her eyes
two grains of salt, her hands held out
      for our embrace. Could we refuse
a hesitant child, the one that in fact appeared,
      because were amazed, fatigued, or shy,
or would we stoop and, heart-stopped, anyway
      gather her into our arms?

The Caul

For my Mother

After a war like that they must have known
nothing was certain—certainly nothing

they privately desired, when simply to wish
more than a life to all meant overreach,

but still, being what she was, at Tilbury, the docks—
February 1919 by memory's acoustic—

on a troop ship from Alexandria,
at full tide drawing to its berth at noonday,

the rails packed with fellows bellowing as one
some ditty like "My darling Clementine,"

she scanned the crowd on the wharf,
face after face upturned, and knew no one
and was unknown,

those on the dock seeing only red faces and O
mouths, hers included, joining her parlor contralto

to the single thousandfold roar. Lost
too her enormous effort, now she was cast away
on the shores of this benighted estuary

far from the waves on Manly Beach and the sun,
and her sisters, and her old sure lover, no one

to meet her. After bitter Greek winters under canvas,
nursing the wounded and malarial, after the deaths and chaos,

wrong-footed. And saw him all at once, full stop:
the hero she had captured, staring up

past her smiles and waves, a stranger
in shabbiest tweeds, whom she felt nothing for.

In the blue light below deck
the unlived years had gone bad, in the triple bunk,
with shit, vomit, urine, sweat. I think

she'd have wept at such things, and this was worse.
But I am imagining. All I truly know is,

while cranes hoisted kit in great nets
and orderlies toted her trunk ashore, panic

struck her. Then she was met and embraced
and they went off and got married,

and no one knew of the hitch till she told
a niece, on a visit home years later, who spoke of it when old.

Inconsequence. Episode in a long story,
her doubt my diamond, my caul

kept for its luck, seeing she was finally cut
into the pack after all, and dealt.

Plymouth, *1945*

It could have been worse.
I'd missed my train on purpose

to meet my mother and say goodbye,
believing I mightn't be back for years.

Oh, folly, *folie de grandeur!* The next train ran late,
jammed with troops and dimly lit,

after eight hours entering Plymouth—midnight,
blacked out, bombed out, imaginary port

of embarcation for war. Shouts
of goodbye: the world emptied out;

a hiss and jolt and the slam
of doors and the reek of the spent engine.

So: a night by a gas fire tasting of metal
and the whispering tea-urn of the Salvation Army?

Rather pat with open palms the grid
of gritty brick walls that led

to the shut-fast Y and peal the dim bell.
Two women opened up and gave me hot milk

in the kitchen, while they watched, dependable,
hands in lap, and I drank like a calf from a pail.

My uniform skirt was covered with stains.
They looked and said nothing, for which I was grateful.

In the morning the sun shone,
I went on my way to my fleet air arm station

believing I'd understood something,
which I hadn't. I arrived as I went on doing,

in an aftermath, when principle
turned awkward, and the air hazed with rebellion.

Passion

The passion of mourning I entered maturity with
was sullen, erotic, and atheist.

"So he hasn't written? Just as well."
Without knowing him, my mother could tell.

She liked to play the malign goddess,
whipping up adverse storms and thwarting Zeus,

but a third of the earth was burned,
a third of mankind murdered,

a third of the sea turned to blood—
what did she have to work on, or complain of,

but her glimpse of a single longed-for thing
that might not want to be longed for, with my longing

vaster always than explanation.
When the truth came quietly into a crowded room

months later, it couldn't be hailed, or cried out for,
its features being already far too familiar—

and the demobbed man who gave me the news
only looked at me kindly, and was incurious.

I said at home: "I heard he was killed."
My mother barely paused. "Perhaps it's just as well."

"But only twenty-eight, and after five years of war,
accidently killed? That's not unfair

for a real hero, one of the best,
as everyone said? Don't you think it's a waste?"

That was the fact I thought might
convince her, but *fact* she would never admit.

So then I left her, unacknowledged,
and in private clung to my rags,

his birdwing smile, and enchanting air of belief
in me—too soon at odds with grief.

Finn's People

landed and waited for him
    till the moors darkened
and the seas grew thick.
    After centuries, absentmindedly
and thinking all the while of Finn,
    they took off their old grey heads
and threw them to cap a nearby hill
    so high and deeply nothing could take root.

They trooped then, headless,
    down the path to an unroofed place,
settled their feet in the turf
    side by side in a ring
and addressed themselves to the future.
    By the time Finn came
they'd have turned to stone.
    He must have grieved, unpunctual Finn,
to find a set of slabs
    that once would have got up to bow
and a cairn of heads
    no longer able to weep.

"Finn's People," Pobull Fhinn, is the name given to a standing stone circle near the cairn of
Barpa Langass, North Uist, in the Western Isles of Scotland.

At the Géricault Exhibition

i. The Hussar

The stallion rears up, his forehoofs primed to strike
any assailant who dares approach on foot.
He knows that he behaves as he's been taught.
We think that he is bred to be heroic.
The rider stands in the stirrups, very like
his horse: a beauty, an aristocrat,
perfectly turned out and well equipped, but
not aware as yet he plays with magic.

Crowds bunch and melt before the dazzling paint.
They know it makes them drab, and how for youth
such stylishness and war go hand in hand,
how action magnifies some little truth;
how real death will soon explode a gun
and toss this jewel in the undergrowth.

ii. Cart-Horses

Grand and benevolent, but simple like children
roughly reared and fed and taught their trade
and place, that's all, they have their great heads skewed
over their shoulders to see the artist who draws them.
They're on their way to work, one day in London
in 1820, led by their carters, who did
not see either what merited Géricault's lucid
and loving assessment, since they were so common.

Who'd guess that they would vanish from streets
so soon in our time?—the smell of their manure,
the clangor of their hoofs on granite sets,
their skids and snorts, their heaving musculature
vanished, while hussars and their mounts still parade
jingling in procession at the tourist hour.

iii. The Kleptomaniac

He's clearly mad. It shows in his intensity,
lit from within like a projector that's jammed
and overheating. He sees nothing and
he's not shaken by the painter: or did he,
when all was finished, walk around to see
his features in the paint? And was it a cure
to recognize himself, and to become aware
that he was recognized and challenged as a spy?

As for the painter, clearly a man possessed
by the subject's passion, he saw the nothing seen
in the fixed eyes, the horrors of distaste
in the worn mouth. He painted dereliction
as if, near death himself, he found expressed
despair as lunatic as it was human.

Missing

That afternoon, midwinter, yawn
of gloom and damp,
lapsed—collapsed
five and a half hours
into a three-mile walk

and the star
who stepped as light as a dance,
Annie the walker,
shot into the void a self
no bigger than a pellet—

Annie, where
were you, where?
Mother and brother
called into the wind
the sound

of her name, they searched
the night's ditches,
four dark pubs, three dark churches,

two village halls, the better hotel,
the banktop tearoom
shut up after Christmas,

the simple necessary road
empty, no good
to her, oblivious
under the porch light
on the remote ridge farm,

hair dripping under her cap,
clothes wet black,
boots clogged with mysterious mud,
across her face recognition
drifting, alien, diffident, glad.

THE ENGAGEMENT

Prothalamion

Hundreds of times have I passed briskly down Stonegate
by the shop where your grandmother's mother
might have naturally halted and strayed

toward its high-waisted dresses and deep skirts
(revelations of ankle and boot): you shot into it
yesterday, shouldering my scruples aside. You bought

a wedding dress in wild silk and a momentous hat—
finest Italian straw and a whirl of tulle.
We wept when we saw you, customers, shop girls and I,

not only because of the price. Great-grandmother's miniature
came sharply to mind. Dead at forty, she left ten daughters
and a confused memory of "eyes like stars."

Moreover, I felt sorry, amid the rejoicing,
for the old blue jeans and the brother's shirt
left in the fitting room, with their smell of tobacco and sweat,

and the shattered book on t'ai chi in one pocket
and the way you would always turn contemptuous
from your marvelous eyes in the glass.

The Fire

One time in particular, after night class,
I saw the woods on fire not a mile from home,
a hundred yards in, on the verge of a field,

sheets of flame flapping as though in a gale.
I got out of the car and heard cracking and splintering,
and winced at the yell of light, and felt

heat suckling my hair, and smelled
the nursery hygenics of pine.
There wasn't a soul about.

Home, I tapped in the alarm. Perhaps
they already knew, but the fire-officer,
bright as a star: "Thanks, we're on our way!"

What happened, I never found out:
screaming sirens, dashing engines, tankers,
hoses, men beating down flames, smolders, ash?

Or nothing. Impertinence, classed as a false alarm?
The mind jams. This nothing more,
this inability to inquire: it happens to me also

when I think of marriage, mine and others',
imagining what you look forward to,
whether it works, and is happy or unhappy.

Fact

Nevertheless, nevertheless: unmitigated fact—
self-righteous squire—stands in the path
shouting it's his, every damned acre, with no rights of way,

and though I laugh once safe, and know how skeptical
I've every right to be, and let my rambling thoughts make fun
of fact, unmitigated fact, nevertheless, nevertheless,

since once I looked for prehistoric stones,
famous monoliths, supposed to be down a lane,
saw sycamores and telephone poles, scaffolding, some fields,

but not the stones, and sat in the car half-wild,
until the sun came out, and dark fell on the wheel,
and I saw the vast stone overhead,

and there, across the wheat, beheld the next,
and then a third, twenty-foot-high at least, massive,
full of mystery: may fact give you such a marriage.

Re-Make

Certain things pain me even now.
Even now, the years tipped out, a rim of salt remains.
Nightly, at three or four o'clock,

a motorbike trundles through my head
bearing two men, both rigid with laughter.
Daft ercs, they're both drunk.

The rider has extricated from the hospital
the pillion passenger with his leg in a cast,
and they're on their way back to their ship.

The one with his leg stuck out,
his name's still with me. Why remember
this titbit he told me? Where's his whole life?

That lover of yours limps into the room
and I'm appalled. No knowing what may happen
to you. Certain things pain me even now.

The Unraveling

That one time, I knew he was pushing his luck.
I sat at the stoplight and saw you both pass,
him with his limp and you at his side, like

Oedipus blinded by his own hand, the blessed Antigone
his guide. Wrong, though, this man could see,
and no, he felt no remorse, but looped your wrist

with a thong of forefinger and thumb, and, cheek
of the fellow, hitched himself on to your belt,
and rested a hand on your neck.

Why didn't he take one end of a stick
and have you at the other to pull him along
so you'd plod together like one animal?

My life, I thought, had fallen into misuse,
while looking at you both.
I felt hanged by the neck like that hapless

Jocasta, from a lamp, in her own palace.
I turned on the wipers to unfog the view
and jetted some water over the glass.

I can't say the view improved. Where had you gone?
The roads ran out, and citizens appeared
and cut Jocasta down. I put the car in gear.

The Con-Man

At the very last moment: "How dare you!" and so on.
The fabulist advances, with his limp, and his load of years,
and his manly broken smile and clutch of promises—

a diamond and ruby ring, honeymoon in the Maldives,
the Azores, or Caracas, an M.G. of your own, a Victorian house
by the river, in the bishop's village, a garden at the back,

a vine in a greenhouse, an orchard, a thicket of raspberries.
When you lay on a sunny bank and closed your eyes,
careless of life, "My treasure!" he exclaimed, and you were all,

all, all his wealth. That boast again! "Oh, but . . . " and worse.
He never buys a drink, or pays a bill. He's on relief.
He was never at Entebbe,

never crashed in Venezuela, his leg
wasn't hurt in saving passengers and crew,
the girls he "adopted" were his very own.

The truth comes cranking in. At the very last moment:
"I cannot believe a word."
This will have been the year we called the police.

If only I'd clobbered the creature and broken his back.
If only we hadn't been glad you were glad.
Again and again we murmur: "This is ridiculous!"

Let It Be

Everything can wait. People can wait,
and baths, and the wearing of clean clothes
freshly ironed and hung, and the use of the brush and comb.

Display can wait, and the raising of eyelids,
and murmuring, "Good morning!" "Good night!"
"I am grateful": expensive words now.

And the house, with its armament
of pots and pans, and its ovens and stoves,
its brushes and dusters and buckets of suds:

Let dirt accumulate there, and letters, and the flash
of the answering machine, fax, e-mail, the lot.
Let ash lie in the fireplace, let leaves pile up

in doorways, let windows buzz with flies and dim
with their dottle, let beetles walk with the silverfish
on the kitchen floor, and grubs breed in blankets and gutter.

For you've reached the end of your time. Nothing matters.
At least, nothing matters to you, though the mason nods
through his Perspex mask at you as he chips his stone

and the ploughman fast in the tractor cabin lifts
at the headland the enormous eightfold blades of his plough,
turns, and engages the rig, and mouths at you and grins.

Time and Again

Time and again I'm Demeter, afield on foot
in winter, in search of a daughter, or even her footprint,
or wisp of her skirt stuff in the bare hedge,

aplod round wood and field, hill and farm, moor and ridge,
with the occasional whistle, or coo-ee, designed not to enrage,
vulnerable as she'd be after Hades' world.

Of course, though, it's winter: therefore she isn't here.
If she were here, it would be spring. A fact simple to remember,
but I forget routinely and drive her wild.

Part of my mind also agrees, in deep hell she is queen
and walks freely and is witty and kind. I see
her radiant among the shades. So much the worse for me,

when I search her out in the bright sun of winter
believing she's lost. Let me remember the appropriate season—
that, and her old cry of "Back off, Mother!"

In the Night

Even as we slept, we became aware of
tearing and munching of grass,
luscious guzzlings and snorts and gasps.
Then came a foldyard cough.

We awoke. Three in the morning
and a handful of stars in the very top
of the tall black window.
Annihilation, eyelids down, not terminus.
Dying, shall I hold you thus?
Pain, is that you? Pain? Pain, is it,

who keeps me alive and out of control?
Who was it said I was too calm,
when all the cheer-up signs were wrong?
Flags, bands, parades, balloons,
even betrothal to the queen?

If it was you, you'll be the death of me.
Such moans and wringing of hands!
I mean to be a hundred and one
and always look after you, Pain.

Annihilation, though, is no excuse.
Even with open lids I just can't see.
What though the scene was much the same,
still dark and still Colonus,

the old one and the girl
pretended all was well. At the signal
the old one was carried off,
the girl took up her story,
the famous horses went on eating grass.

New Poems

The Pebble

To date, it lies at the door, your pebble with the hole in it,
together with little fingers from the island of Ossabaw,
shoe-button ambers from the Whitby beach,
the San Diego stone with the petrified worm trails,
sea-glass from Narragansett, the big ammonite
I took from a moorland wall. Your pebble alone
aches with recognition.

To date, the rosemary I rooted
at each side of the door has grown by two feet,
Albertine that marvelous rose has climbed to the eaves,
and the clematis Montana wreathed window after window.
It was soon after you returned from the Gulf
I planted the lot, in an effort to anchor my life.
Look how well they have done by that little stone
which aches with recognition.

Admit it all the while to be nothing but a stone
that the seas have tumbled till the middle was run
through: you wore it on your finger like a wedding ring
the day you came home from the war in the Gulf.
Bernini's marble Saint Teresa was something of the same—
pierced by a laughing angel's spear in a long swoon
of bliss and agony. I know the feeling well.
The O mouth in the stone cries out, you start to die a little.

A Vacant Lot, Boston

The ground is gray,
the color of the moon through rain
and sugared underfoot
probably like the moon,

and that stadium
bobbing in the distance
somewhat out of focus
may be a moon-mooring station

on which the moon might settle,
golfball on a tee
or a round blimp netted
in case it blew away.

Up the hill in the ex-Christian church
Zen Buddhists in unison
bellow and brandish
wooden swords in a dance.

In the churchyard flourish
their zinnias, carrots, lettuce,
sunflowers, marigolds, basil,
and, among red dragons, cabbage.

In the lot there's only chicory
in crevices, more root than stem,

filaments of silvery string
and faded blue flowers.

That bitter root with its papery bloom,
it's what we'd use
for famine coffee and famine flowers
if we were on the moon.

A Telephone Call

The raindrop was waiting to drip, the bell to sound,
signals to change, the plane to land,

and the slow movement of ordinary causes
ground on till the telephone rang. "Hullo, who's this?"

A tearful kid. "Lady, are you married?"
Everything stopped, and the line went dead.

A joke? You serious? Surely set up.
As married woman I'd have gushed with hope

and hoped that was enough, my role
preaching a nondespair. "Darling? Angel?"

I'd have said. "If you find yourself with child,
if you must face survival's

minimum, listen to this strategy, quack, quack . . . "
and heard the kid explode. Too slick

by half. I'd know she knew it all.
Her modus operandi was pure hell.

She'd string me up, rake memories
back to flame, reverse causation: wasn't

that him still, terror, over there, wearing his sweetheart grin?
So what'll it be this time, just for fun?

Sandals

"These sandals?" I mimicked surprise.
"Very very comfortable, yes,

not elegant." I might have confessed there and then,
but sidestepped and said they were German,

"and yet don't you think they look Roman?"
"If they were Roman, they'd have a thong

round the ankle," said Maurice.
Oh. And it swam into my mind that Arminius

(or Hermann) in 9 A.D. led a German army
to annihilate three Roman legions, causing

their general Varus to fall on his sword.
The avenging army of Germanicus was almost disappeared

five years later, also by Hermann. So Germany
never became Roman, which was why . . .

Anyway, all
looked at my sandals,

German not Roman, thongless, comfy.
No one repeated *elegant,* nobody spoke of *money.*

Flax

Walking through a fieldful of flowers
brighter blue than blue eyes,
I'm mindful of the man who flew
his microlight from Bristol to Oxford
by way of fields of flax—
in July, at noon, so many blue
squares on a green board:
he memorized the pattern, the lie
of diagonals colored blue
for easy return.

But at dusk the petals closed
and he had to fly a gray-green line
a bit left of the sun: southwest dead ahead,
then a space under the buzz of his engine,
which duly cut out at the Bristol Channel.

Homeless

"I've a coat might fit you. And shoes,"
said my mother. "What size do you take?"
His toes lay podgy and pink
in the gap between boot sole and upper.
He sat by the kitchen fire
in the stiff snotty coat, small
and bearded like our king,
with a slab of bread and butter
in one hand, a cup of tea in the other.
He was agreeable, I think.
His eye smiled under its lid.

"He'll have a house at home," said Lily.
"Condemned, it is likely,
with doors and windows soft with damp.
Beetles and silverfish will scatter like shot
when his wife brings in the lamp,
rats twitter in the walls.
For him you could say it's better on the road."

So many green bells to sleep under
sounding on the edge of the field,
so many bluebells swelling under the trees.
He might lie down in a hedge
that creaked with drought and mice.
He could easily sleep in a barn.
Outside there'd always be stars.

When he left by the back door
I wished I had spoken. Last week
I saw him, much younger and stronger,
holed up in a portal, with a dog this time,
a step from the lights and the traffic,
miles from the ditch and the wood
and the barn, and the stars,
the same I have never forgotten,
the same I can only describe.

January

Fog thumbs the wrinkles,
fuzzes roofs, telephones,
road lines, steeples,
skylines, brightnesses,
smudges the ends,
blots sheep, blobs a lit window,
the lights of an oncoming car;

varnishes paint on iron gates also,
polishes slates on roofs,
waxes pantiles,
butters tarmac,
beads the loft of wool on a coat,
frizzes hair, spangles eyelashes.

Trees that stood by the wall
rigid as shotguns
begin to rust and melt;
the walls themselves
blur and moss over.

And it is cold—as cold as Jericho—
it might as well be Jericho:
big solitary stones in fields
dislodged as though by trumpets—
the face of things remote,
a friend's whose thoughts are elsewhere,

a bad slow blocked time
when nothing works,
when zero begins to repeat
zero, zero, zero.

Sex

The horrors of abatement
and a ticking off
were the straight results of my childish statement
that trees don't have a sex.

Most do, the teacher insisted, and some have both at once.
Lex-
icographers, note: *clone*
entered the language in 1903 and still wasn't current
when I noted our poplars had only one parent.
They were in fact clones, adventitious.
One got a disease, all died of it. Whereas
most trees, like my furious teacher with her red face and me,
were the fruit of marrying out.
In each of us, strangers had come together.
Not what we knew, but what we didn't know
gave us immunity.

If only I'd been given that word *clone*
to play with, what a comfort it would have been
when men, so different from me, whistled down the wind!

The Sleeve

You took your arm out of its sleeve last night
with a sigh like a train
about to exit
from York's Victorian station,
arc of cast iron, plate glass and air—
leaving so quietly it seems to disappear,
so brilliant that lunette
of expeditionary light
beyond the platforms,

so bright that hand of yours
entering the arc
of the lamp, the tweedy semi-dark
of the sleeve abandoned and falling to the floor
as a building might crumple
in the soundless shockwave
following an explosion.

1919

She was explosive, had to be handled
    with care, or avoided; she told lies
as it suited, never admitted a doubt.
    After thirty-five years of her absence
I've peered below and I've seen
    still radiant ore in the workings,
and have quickly withdrawn
    to pitface and daylight and grass.

Repeat it, however: in that wintry Bloomsbury room
    in the run-up to marriage, she dreams
malarial dreams; dreams and drowns in grief,
    cries out for company, oranges,
clean sheets, aspirin, tea, her bevies
    of sisters, the Murray River, past lovers:
the maid creaks past in the hotel corridor
    and she starts to get better.

A letter says here she rode in a box taxi
    to a church full of his flowers;
a brother of his attended, witnesses came off the street.
    She entered glittering and alone.
His womenfolk's metronome ticked
    they were the salt of the earth, the elect,
Israel's lost tribe, and she laughed. She was pretty,
    kick-started the rest. So he began to smile.

The Job

In Trenton, New Jersey,
I went to work in the state museum
because we were short of money.
I had a dirty little office
full of lists: lists
of those with millions to give,
lists of quite ordinary art lovers,
lists of how much they gave, for what
work of art, or for what work.
There was a safe, a typewriter, a telephone,
besides the files to hold the lists.
I was supposed to drum up donations
and keep the books. It seemed easy.
Everyone was hopeful of me.

My office window overlooked
the Delaware beyond the car park,
a big broad pebbly river,
with isolated bars of willow and alder
and little birches rooted among stones.
Along the far bank lay the old canal
where barges used to ply
before the railroad came.
To the right there was a bridge,
its surface made of metal grid
that made the traffic purr.

(Sing, Delaware, forever and forever,
and you, bridge, hum
as traffic passes to and from
leafy grassy Pennsylvania.)

The museum building was new,
white marble, a flat roof, lots of plate glass
where light flooded in, and rain at times
(you could smell the mildew:
there had been a lawsuit).
To one side stood the state library,
a bit older, and the state capitol,
from the past century, complete
with gold-leaf dome and Grecian portico:
three baubles along the neglectful river,
three separate bright ideas.
And beyond some car parks and their bushes
stood the low pioneer's house
of Trent, a merchant, father of the city,
dwarfed under banks and offices,
like someone bereaved or foreign,
or using an idiom no longer in fashion.

Driving into the city, you passed through
yet another idea, a dream in someone's sleep.

(The old traffic lights look out under iron shades or lids.
Their posts have several bands that bulge about the middle.
There's one to each corner of the crossing,
not centered on arms overhead. Too close,
and you can't see if the light's turned green.
The roadway's curb is chipped, the surface pocked,
pothole after pothole furnished with a light

that here and there time has extinguished,
that flails with stones when wheels lurch through.
Only the roadman's lights spread a little warmth.
The quiet canal is buttered with plastic; chickenwire fences
give shoots of sumac a hold, bindweed in paving stones.
Tarpaper shingle and breezeblock shanties
crawl up to a rank hotel sixteen storys high;
its concrete drips black, paint peels off its wooden doors.
Unscripted areas flow round its walls. Clouds butt on roofs.
Snow on the road, cold at windows stuffed with newspaper.
In the hotel, the stink of old cigars. Almost nothing left.

Look, though, at that once lovely house:
verdigris stains the brick under the gutter breaks,
slates have slipped from the roof, the front is cracked across.
The unpainted cornices have rotted under the eaves.
The white wood portico needs jacking up,
and a few stone treads have worked askew on the stair.
Finials are bent, and so are fleur-de-lys tips
to cast-iron railings trimming the small court.
After a century's use, the white courtyard gate
no longer weds its latch to the opposing notch.
But a woman dignified and ancient as the night
is rocking on the porch at five on a warm day.
Two black and tan coonhounds lie tethered in the yard.
Her washing is pinned on lines hung under the buttonwood.
Children are playing hopscotch on the sidewalk stone.
And now they dance in a ring, grasping each other's hands:
She leans forward and claps, pricked in the eye of love.)

It was curious, in this city center,
to mark the absence of stores,
though there were burnt-out buildings

that might have held stores.
There was that big hotel,
there weren't showrooms
or builder's yards or garages
or radio stations or TV studios,
and where people lived,
except in the slums, I couldn't see either.
I couldn't see even where they worked.
Presumably they didn't work,
those who lived in the slums:
that's why they were there.
So where was everyone else?—
The museum was staffed, of course,
but where was its public?
Or did the building come first,
was desire for it to happen later,
as appetite comes with eating?
Heavens, once in place, did it mortify
the people who never wanted it?—
who didn't know what to do with it?
Certainly it was meant to stiffen
the flabby municipal conscience:
priceless as it was, with no street value,
it confronted us all. What did we want,
if not this? Self-congratulation
among New Jersey legislators?
Certainly not a single senator
came visiting for pleasure.

Every day as I drove in to work
I wondered what art
reflected the dead factories

along the railroad or the canal—
places difficult of access now,
through brick canyons or smothered alleys
along sleeves of grass,
along highways speckled with trash,
over humped bridges
that cricked the backs of cars;
what art reflected people on the street,
the men waiting for the liquor store to open,
the children walking to school
clean and pretty, holding hands.

And I had no sooner begun work
in my cleaned-up little office than the patrons
of the museum held an evening party
to launch a special exhibition,
and on the way out, in the dark,
I walked into flashing lights:
two girls ran between the cars,
one in clipping hip-high boots
and a tiny leather skirt. She got away—
the other was caught and tossed
over the front of a car and frisked—
more huge-bellied police
idly moving round the car,
caps rammed over their eyes,
nightsticks surging over massive hips.
Blue lights revolved, a siren
breathed low, a beast
barely held in check.

The dangers, apparently, were many.

I was told to keep car doors locked
as I drove in to work, because
a woman had recently been
forced off the road and raped
by a gang of youths.
Even though the rape turned out to be
her ex's answer to her request for
seven million dollars alimony,
still it looked arbitrary.
The woman who ran the museum shop
was mugged in broad daylight by a child.
A purse left in my office
was lifted by someone
who drove to Merrill Lynch and cashed
two thousand dollars on a payment card.

And often people spoke
of Mary-Jo, a wealthy patron,
who'd moved into a little restored house,
an old house in the center,
to show her faith in the city—
a blonde woman she was,
a plump and lively woman.
They told how one night a man forced a window
and raped her. A month later—
seeing the window still broken—
he came back and killed her
with an axe and a knife and a hammer.

And one day Sam was sick,
sweet-hearted Sam, the messenger
who glided with winged feet
from office to office calling

"God mornin'! Hah you?"—
dispensing mail like gifts.
Sam the invincible, sick?
I'd visit him on my way home, I said;
at which his boss went wild.
"Man, ya crazy? They'll kill ya
soona looka ya, nice lady like you.
Sam, he don' wan' nothin' happen t' ya.
Ya don' do no good tryin' sumthin'
like that. Sam, he be back in a day a two.
Man, don' ya visit nobody there!"

So I didn't, craven.

Six busloads of small children,
six yellow buses and two hundred little people
in yellow shirts, sweetly ruddy and shiny,
healthy and in good voice—

how can the art stand it?
The day is hot, under the pearly trees,
on the worn grass, on the concrete paths.
The statues are hot to the touch.
Some children smooth them with starfish hands,
smooth and dreamily pat.

"Freeze!" shouts the teacher. "Freeze!
Freeze!" The children hush slowly
like leaves turning white in the wind.
"It's time to eat your lunch!"
Nowhere to eat in the museum,
nowhere to sit down

(the director's afraid of crumbs,
the director's afraid of vagrants).

So the children eat outside
on worn grass, under pearly trees;
and after they've gone in,
tattered people close in
to forage in the trash bins
for bread crusts and half apples,
some to eat instantly, some
to thrust into pockets.
(Just so at receptions,
unfortunates infiltrated
the crowd of guests, and toured the artworks,
mouths crammed with tiny sandwiches).

Inside the air is cool, and painting
bright as a rainbow, could be real rainbow,
painted flowers could be real.
Children, they are not real:
feel it, they are so chilly,
they are so necessary, they're supreme.
They mean almost everything.
They are cold, of necessity,
deep-frozen stuff, endurables, constructs.
Children, do not touch.

The children go whooping
through the galleries:
they stare at a painting and then dance on.
They buy sodas from machines
and trinkets from the shop
and then they pile into buses,

which buzz off neatly like six bees.
Silence takes its time coming back.

I walked through the galleries too.
It was the authentic I wanted, not consolation.
I tried smelling hay in painted fields,
I tried hearing bells from a painted church,
tried feeling like Juan Gris, when he portrayed
oil refineries, or Georgia O'Keeffe
viewing Hoboken at roof-level.
I tried playing a sculptor's piano
made of bedsprings and tissue paper,
but the nearest I could come
to the real was a broken column
set in the middle of the gallery floor
with its capital to one side and
its base on the other.

I never thought art existed
to do you good, on principle.
Instead, it drew you in,
into itself, so inside art
you'd feel as the artist did.
Which changed you too,
both in yourself and in
your private world.

Made to be secondary,
a therapy or ploy,
art filled me with gloom.
Art here seemed secondary,

to the world outside,
or to a private world
I could not recognize.
No one said as much.
I don't think that anyone knew
how powerful the threat was outside,
twirling its guns,
nor how remote and silly
and secondary art became
because of it.

Perhaps the museum
was all too clear and bright
to allow mysteries
like the mysteries of art;
too aboveboard, too naive.
Outside was fear,
which couldn't be portrayed
except by failure.
Here love of art tossed real love away,
and was so diminished by the act
as to prove incapable.

I lasted about a year in the museum,
working hard to raise money,
and doing quite well in all,
although unskilled at bookkeeping.
Then someone offered me something better,
and the director said I had outgrown the job,
and was happy to let me go.

(Sing, Delaware, past the capitol,
sing, by dome and portico,
have the museum cry io,
Trenton io, io, io,

while the heavy north-south trains
crawl over the creaking railroad bridge,
sing where your rivery old heart is,
by your abandoned factories,

by the canals where heron fish,
where the sometime wharfs collapse,
sweetly, sweetly, sing!)

Why Poetry: An Essay

"I want you to be dependent," my mother said. I had been telling her what I wanted to do when I grew up.

Dependent? Forced to stick with her, Mummy's little girl, every secret mocked, exploited, playfully indulged? No, worse, far worse. She meant me to be a fine lady and keep a fine house. The key to this horrible enterprise, it became clear, was marriage to a rich man, whose dependent I would be just as I was hers as a child. He would ensure that I'd never have to do a hand's turn, unlike her, who was not married to a rich man and consequently was busy in the house from morning to night. So my husband would be rich and would dote and I'd be charming.

I wept. I knew I'd never be charming. I didn't want to be charming, I wanted my own way. In any case, we knew no rich people.

"And you shouldn't learn to cook, so your husband will have to provide you with plenty of servants."

"I shall never marry," I said.

She stopped laughing. "You're going to grow up into one of those mannish Highland women like your Aunt Mary." Aunt Mary was the formidable matron of Glasgow Royal Infirmary. "Or a B.A.! B.A.s are dirty!"

At the age of nine, permitted to attend school at last, I found several B.A.s, some of them charming women. I discovered other degrees, attached to women doctors, solicitors, dentists, local government officials. They weren't dirty at all. But there was always some grain of truth in my mother's prejudices, and I realized in time that it was the neglected houses of the B.A.s that she objected to, from the unsupervised maids who served tea in greasy china and didn't whiten the doorsteps or polish the brass on the front door, to their families—the husbands with ragged collars and filthy cuffs and stained ties and unpolished shoes, the children with woebegone faces and uncertain manners. My mother herself regarded her domestic life as her accomplishment. You could see it the moment you walked over the threshold and saw her tomato-red carpet and her flowers and gleaming silver and old oak furniture she'd carried out of derelict farmhouses and repaired and polished, the pewter plates like moons on the dresser, the brass fenders and scuttles and brass-topped pokers and tongs sunning by the hearth. You'd know it if you ate her good food on good plate, her bread, her cakes, her pies, her spiced beef, her trifle.

So much style was meant to delight and challenge and blackmail. If you like it, love me and copy me, and I will exact your sorrow for the way I slave to create this picture of calm and comfort and pleasure: that was the set of her mind. I turned aside, not permitted to say that the house was boring. I couldn't think how she'd come to the conclusion that it was just the thing for me. Anyway, I didn't see why she was so devious, especially when I compared her schemes with the big aboveboard deals of my father. If the house pleased her, why was she always complaining, about the maids, the modesty of our income, and her hard work?

Then her campaign medals turned up in a drawer. Medals? Decorations, with their important grosgrain ribbons in moiré reds and blues dangling from a clasp, in a leather box from Spink of Piccadilly, like a soldier's. Fingering them reflectively, my father spoke of life-and-death times when she'd been far from her Australian home, nursing in Greece during the Great War. After such suffering and such labor, life as I knew it should have been pleasant. But she didn't use that heroic and admirable time as a touchstone, she simply put it behind her. She told me it was terrible, and sighed with real grief, and that was it. She wouldn't talk about it. It took me years to discover the truth. She didn't refer to it because she didn't want me to copy her. She said mysteriously that she was ashamed, and I could see that she was being perfectly honest for once. It was hard on her to be ashamed of having been brave, I thought. Yet even in that she was illogical and untrustworthy. "Your mother is a great snob," my father said. She thought nice women didn't run off to the war and nurse soldiers, hear foul language, live in mud and squalor. Of course I could not agree, because in this one episode I found her quite wonderful, and whether she was nice or not didn't matter.

Recently an ancient cousin has died, unlocking a hoard of letters, photos, and hearsay. Her daughter has also referred me to a book in which photographs of my mother appear, showing her sitting outside a bell tent with two other nurses. She carries a white umbrella and wears a hat with a brim and a white dress to the ankles, with little boots showing underneath. The garden party look is totally misleading; to it, my mother has sacrificed the truth in the shape of more brutal and less flattering photographs, which she destroyed. The Australian nursing unit to which she is attached has been sent to the 50th British General Hospital at Kalamaria, near Salonika in northern Greece. It is August 1917, two years after the disaster at Gallipoli in which so many Australian soldiers died, and my grandfather has permitted her to leave her private hospital in Sydney and volunteer for service only because he has no sons to send to the war. Nursing is still considered a vulgar occupation, and my privileged mother has had to battle for her training: now at last she is to be vindicated.

The 50th, I have learned through my cousin, was a hut hospital. Other hospitals nearby were in tents. By October 1917 heavy rains caused floods that coursed through the tents and reduced the sites to knee-deep mud. By late November snow fell, driven by gales. The only heating in the wards and the nurses' quarters, mostly under canvas, came from the little traditional charcoal-burning braziers of the Ottoman Empire. Australians didn't know such cold existed. Moreover in August Salonika had suffered a devastating fire which left a huge population of homeless starving people. The docks were so dislocated that medical and food supplies were periodically cut off, and thieves kept raiding the nurses' quarters. There weren't many battle casualties. The beds were full of British and Australian soldiers suffering from dysentery, typhoid, tuberculosis, influenza, and malaria. Many died. My mother too was ill. Her weight sank to under a hundred pounds. She had a bout of malaria in a cold London hotel in winter, 1919, when she was quite alone.

And yet—this is the moral, the punchline—she met my father in Salonika. He was a doctor, seconded to the 50th General Hospital from a hospital ship that had worked the Dardanelles. He was a handsome good man, shy to the end of his days. She liked him, she fancied him, she proposed marriage, and thank goodness he accepted. He told me of her proposal only forty-five years later, when she died. When I laughed with pleasure he was taken aback.

There was only one threat to the idyll, told to the ancient cousin when she was young, and eventually passed on to me. When her ship docked at Tilbury in 1919 after the voyage from Greece, my mother looked down from the deck and saw on the quay the man with whom she was to spend the rest of her life, a man no longer in his beautiful uniform but in a dreadful suit, for whom she felt absolutely nothing. For this creature she was abandoning father, sisters, home and country, a fiancé, friends, and independence? In fact the marriage was a happy one, and my father soon found a better tailor. After that moment of regret she abandoned the past. Even her childhood became short and far away. She officially forgot the number of her sisters as if it were indecent, she forgot her true age, and the method by which my grandfather made his fortune, and of course the Macedonian campaign and the mud and cold in which so many died far from the noise of battle.

I am pushing a pram to the butcher's, Herr Winkler's, in leafy bourgeois Grunewald in West Berlin. The narrow residential street runs between vast operatic ruins. This is Occupied Berlin nine years after the peace following the Second World War, pre-Wall and post-Air Lift. The boom years are yet to come, but West Berliners observe to each other how fat they are getting.

We cross the footbridge over the tiny Dianasee with its jetties rotting in the water below and its little bandstand for three or four musicians on summer nights in the kaiser's day. Our dachshund Bloom plunges down a bank and flings himself into the still green water for his daily swim. A citizen stops to inform me that swimming is bad for dachshunds. Their backs, it seems, are frail and can be thrown out of kilter by the paddling motion of huge dachshund paws.

"I know," I say. *"Leider."* It seems easier to say so, such is the state of my German. Bloom joins us in a shower of droplets, eager to make a new acquaintance.

"Ach. Ein Dackel der alter Schule!" The citizen beams. There is nothing wrong with Bloom's back after all.

"Swimming seems to make him strong," I venture.

"He should be on a lead," says the citizen. "And where is his official number? You should register him immediately."

Another citizen has paused helpfully. "Foreigners do not need to register their dogs."

"Really?" Both citizens now peer into the pram. More advice follows. the baby kicking and crowing in his nest of blankets and pillows should be wearing bootees. And a hat, a woolly hat. But certainly bootees. A proverb follows. I release a volley of thanks and depart in it.

It twists my soul to feel the object of kindness and at the same time someone belonging to the brutal nation responsible for the ruins and the mountain of rubble cleared from them that was rising in the park. To avoid censure I should follow the incessant advice that perfect strangers feel free to offer me, but I don't because in my mind I feel they should be angry with me, just as I should be angry with them, and the absence of anger on both sides is somehow made tolerable by their unwanted advice and my refusal to heed it. So the dog romps off the lead, the baby goes barefoot and bareheaded. People must recognize without being told that I've crossed into the holy land of matrimony and motherhood and can do no wrong. I am learning to cook, and to be frugal, easy enough, since I've grown up in the war. I study German and attend the remarkable Brecht Theater am Schiffbauerdamm. I write a little poetry and begin another novel. I deal with my husband's terrible depressions, which drag us both to the brink. (How can he be depressed when he is married to me?) Yet we are an anomaly among anomalies, foreigners but German civil servants, exiles while every barracks is crammed with native Germans, refugee Osties from the Russian zone; ex-enemies while a few frail ghosts of prisoners-of-war turn up from camps in Siberia where they have been enslaved for ten years.

The people we know vary from spies and diplomats and soldiers and journalists to the half-Jewish professor who has passed as Aryan and now talks like a freed slave, or the garage mechanic who over a coffee boasts of killing Jews in the Ukraine, or the noble few who have returned from plush exile in America to bring something precious back to the new Germany. They are all unduly representative of something or other, and their differences are earnestly discussed. My husband teaches in the Free University. His colleagues are very old. The students appear middle-aged. One has never seen a cat before. One tells me that in East Germany they wash the linen not once a week but twice a year. They always bring flowers, which they cannot afford, and they do not know when to go home at the end of a party. Their politeness is inhibiting. I long to know them better.

Now I am coming back from the butcher's, the grocer's, the baker's, and the pharmacy, and the pram is full of little parcels. The baby has stopped kicking and lies alert on his pillow looking up at the tree. "He needs bootees," says a citizen, stopping to admire. "A hat too, a woolly hat. You should cover him up. I hope you do not let him play with the dog. Dogs carry disease in their mouths and they lick babies. They are not to be trusted."

"Thank you," I say. I wish there was someone to speak my mind to. I would like to tell someone of my son's birth, but no one wants to hear, not even my husband, whose eyes glaze over at the idea of ecstasy. No one is interested. I should write more poems, a sheaf of poems, but who will read them? Those that get published in England bounce off the political situation. I have no faith in what really cries out for celebration. And my mind is wadded with the complacency of pregnancy and childbirth.

It has to be said, in spite of this picture of frustration, that marriage has cut the cackle. The little career has petered out that began with a pamphlet of novice poetry published through John Wain and the great printer William McCance at Reading University. No more inclusion in anthologies, reduced publication in journals, no more invitations to write reviews, no invitations to read at the old ICA off Piccadilly, no poetry evenings with competent poets at George and Paddy Fraser's in Chelsea; no literary parties where William Empson and Kathleen Raine and Janet Adam Smith are kind to the young; no lunch with Kingsley and Hilly Amis at which they pump me for information about the man I am living with. My novel has been published and Olivia Manning and others have reviewed it generously. But that is that. The baby keeps me at home and prevents me from getting to know German society well enough to use it in a second novel. I do not publish another for forty years. But this is life, I think. My husband has forced me to live.

What is the literary life worth, I ask, missing the bit I knew. Recognition means you write more, for you write to be read, and recognition means readers, and a marketplace to display your wares, and sales if possible, which make possible the creation of more wares. All this subjects the wares to criticism, good and bad. Without such criticism I found myself fumbling in the dark. Similarly, without a familiar and open society to draw from, I was confused, and turned from writing novels to poetry, with its concentrated focus and promise of an end. It was both inspiring and goading to see my friend Nina Bawden publishing a book a year. I liked her ease and conviction. I liked her vulnerability. I liked what she had to say.

During this immense frustration, it took a long time to appreciate the awkward truths of my new life. On the one side, I was living with someone who understood what I was trying to do and who backed me up. He understood the wish to write because he was a writer himself. He made a space for me in the house and in the time of day. But his effort horrified me, it seemed so untoward and unrewarding. Marriage and motherhood, nevertheless, had speeded things up. No more gazing out of the window. Less hesitancy over the right word.

And yet: Despair. He prized me for the wrong things. Frustration made me sick and violent. There was no leisure and no money to buy leisure. Because my husband was my patron, I felt absurd pressure to write as one of a couple rather than as an individual—especially when it became clear that it was marriage that I should write about. I tried not to write any more. Eventually, though, on a visit, I attended a reading in Edinburgh where I heard three distinguished Scots poets read such rubbish from their work that I knew I could do better, and started to write again. But meanwhile I had crossed the divide, the angry divide between the independent woman and the woman kept at home by her babies. Eyeing my old self across the gulf, I am embarrassed. What is she signaling to me, that self-righteous creature over there? Why is she jumping up and down and shouting? I am looking at her deeply stirred and with my mother's eyes.

◎◎

Once or twice my mother has turned up in my poems unbidden. One, called "I Object, Said the Object," I wrote after moving house from Maine to New Jersey with my husband and our nine-year-old son, and our new baby, six weeks old. In less than a month my husband took off on a mission to Europe. The hall was blocked with packing cases. It was August and hellish hot. The well became poisoned in the drought and started to give dark red smelly water. My milk dried up. Our son, a great comfort, went off to his new school and left me with the baby all day. I was due to go back to my work as a medical editor in a matter of weeks. If I had help in the house I don't remember it. I felt I was drowning and my children were drowning with me. Just to drive out to buy bread and milk was a major undertaking. I fell asleep in the middle of the day and lay awake at night. Wandering through the unfamiliar garden in moonlight I picked a small fruit like a plum and chipped a front tooth on its stone. Letters from my husband gathered unread. He had gone first to visit my father—my father, not his. It seemed to me that my husband had taken over my life and left nothing for me, not even my father.

This injustice, as I saw it, was too large and imprecise to protest about. And life was unjust anyway, only denying me briefly what it denied other women for a lifetime. Supposing, though, I had complained to my husband before he left and asked him to abandon his mission: he would say, as he'd said before on earlier fellowships and research trips, did I want him to stay home and rot? And I would reply, as earlier, no, if he didn't see the injustice it was already too late. I was not going to argue about justice and demand fair shares. That was beneath me, I thought. I would manage on my own. Other women did. After all, he should be himself. (If I could not be myself, well, it was better and clearer for one person to be himself than for two people, him and me, to be both lost.)

Suppose I told my husband that I would not be there when he came back. This is what I should have said, according to two of my friends. But where would I go, with my small entourage? I had no relatives to fall back on, and was not sure that I would have used them anyway. My friends certainly didn't bother to offer me a roof. Even if I took all the money out of the bank and left, it wouldn't last long, and what then? How would I go on with my job without my husband's moral and physical support? The children needed a father. I had made vows. And who was going to make love to me? I couldn't think of anyone else I wished to be in bed with. Suppose I told my husband not to come back: he'd come anyway, bursting open the locks and laughing. I imagined myself to be my husband, faced with a weeping accusing wife, tiresomely flouncing and ridiculous. A poem began itself immediately.

To my surprise, the woman I was depicting as a ravening force of nature, one who angered and wore down the narrator (me as husband), became the Muse, she whom though only an occasional visitor in our house I longed to have as permanent guest. After all, the Muse is only a device. One can switch genders to suit. A woman can play the man quite as well as a man can play the woman. A woman imagines men all the time just as much as a man imagines a Becky Sharp or a Portia or Anna Karenina; her act is not so taken for granted, that is all. The poem ended with the woman calmly addressing the narrator (still me as man), and telling him to bring his sheep, his lambs, the unshorn poems, dear to him but strange, down from the hills of his imagination to a place where they are familiar and fearless. The narrator agrees.

Heart-full and grateful then I'll bid them come,
  Their mouths like filmstars' ravaged and remote
  Uttering sounds unchosen, spontaneous, not
    Chidden, flocking,
My lambs, crowding to me, a stranger that says,
"What is it that you want? Is it this? Or this?"

As Freud says, What is it women want?

The narrator here (me) turns into the poet, the woman poet as it happens. The lambs are both her children and her poems. I duly sent off this effort to my husband, then in Paris, hoping to wound him and feeling heartsick. A poem was less important than a human being. So the days passed, and the self I'd objectified as the maenad assumed my mother's face. She was dead by then, and I had no fear of hurting her. She would never have seen herself anyway in what I originally planned as a caricature of myself. There she was, however, in me and also in the Muse, satisfactorily willful and showing her sharp teeth.

Presently my husband replied from Paris. He had not the slightest idea of the true meaning of the poem and its convoluted history and simply congratulated me on it. Ha, what a thick skin he'd got! Strange, though: on some occasions I had shown him poems only to see him turn red and cry, "Thanks very much!" as if I'd kicked him. He had simply taken my meaning too personally—a solecism I thought he'd be immune to.

It is very hard to write from the heart of your marriage. Sylvia Plath did it, at terrible cost. Her accomplishment has made the task seem at least possible, though her marriage was unique. Was mine unique? Why didn't I know more about marriage beforehand? Was it worth the effort to write from the heart of marriage, or are we limited to celebration? To write through difficulty made for better poems than to write through ease, not because I despised the gracefulness of ready language, but because sometimes I didn't know what the difficulty really was. I didn't know its shape, its importance generally, or its habitat in language. I thought, rightly or wrongly, that I had to discover such knowledge through the poem itself. For one thing, such difficulty loaded the work with the life—even my life then, trivialized with meeting the needs of my family and household, and haunted by the demands of my job as an editor of medical publications; and paradoxically tormented by the desire to put my own words on paper. The hurt for the poet in me, that mannikin, was marriage, my excellent marriage. The poem I've referred to, "I Object, Said the Object," represented a first success at getting out of the bog where my feet were stuck. I like to think that things got easier after writing it, but it's taken a lifetime to attach the life to the poetry, and only now that I'm old and have a little leisure and a room of my own, still in my husband's company, do the life and the poetry go along together without falling over every few paces, whipped though they may be by desire.

But what desire is that, I ask myself today, dissatisfied with these rationalizations. Why do I want to write poetry? Surely not just to work things out, nor to solve riddles, nor for health. To sing, then? To record, to celebrate, to play, to have a good time? For all those reasons. The value of definition varies with the need. Long before art, there was necessity. I understood when my parents were disbelieving ("Did John Wain write that for you?") or scandalized ("Oxford has been the ruination of you!") or bored ("Who is this fellow you keep going on about? He's dead, is he? Probably a good thing."). The reason for all that nakedness escaped them, as it does me. They sniffed at the eroticism of my verses with horror, as well they might. Why did I go back over my experience, why not leave it alone. It was no better than dog's vomit, that only a dog returns to. In the same manner, a lady asked what I would write about, because I was too young to have anything to say. She meant that I had no conversation. She may not have meant to be personal, but only to imply that she'd seen a lot herself. Also, the silence of others was criticism in itself. Here, a literary life would have come in useful, as when people told me that they knew my husband had done my work, or at least helped me with it, when the whole point was that he was in opposition. They were used to the idea that women did their husbands' work for them—marking papers, acting as their assistants, and so on. Why not, then, let the husband be equally generous; it's nothing for him (they must have thought), he probably ran it off before breakfast.

Disbelief, as I've suggested, stems primarily from the gaze. What was true of parents' gaze was true of a husband's, or children's, or students'. You have only to imagine Rilke writing his *Duino Elegies* on a campus, his refusal of private ties held against him, his invisible necessity lost, his angels turning away with shielded eyes, to see the advantages of private life in solitude. The private needs of women—poet or plain—tend to be overlooked by the people who are gazing at them. That is particularly striking in the case of Sylvia Plath, whose passion was misinterpreted until Ted Hughes's *Birthday Letters*. And even here some confusion remains over what kind of truth is involved in her poems—the truth of poetry or the truth of who did what to whom.

At least poetry, seen or not, can be practiced in private. Perhaps that explains why women are on the whole better writers than painters or musicians. They can work with a pencil on the back of the scrap of paper, like Emily Dickinson or the Brontës, or even memorize beforehand what they will eventually consign to paper, like Irina Ratushinskaya, who was forbidden writing materials in prison. Painters learn their craft in groups, and musicians rely on public performance. Only poets can work stealthily. Not that they always want to, of course; most would prefer what I have now, a good warm room with plenty of light and space to spread books and papers and leave them lying about till a job is over, and the latest in writing machines. And the assumption in ancient Greece that poetry serves a public need and belongs in the public sphere is a delightful one. No question there of being "difficult" and "élitist." Poetry belonged to everyone and everyone appreciated it. Poetry for us doesn't have much meaning until its deeply subjective nature is clear and the authorship of poems attested with photos and little biographies like this one.

And yet—such is poetry's drive toward the impersonal—I once believed poems spoke for themselves. I hated asking for backers. I left unsigned poems on people's tables, something I now see was a girlish thing to do. My husband's assumption that my poems were about him, I have called a solecism, and it shocked me. But I was present and he knew me, and that was his unspoken excuse. Once I read a poem before a university audience about the demands of a house and family and how they came into conflict with my own private work, and I tried to refer to the infinite riches brought by a husband and children which gave rise to staggering contradictions. Afterwards a professor, brushing aside mention of love and riches as so much humbug, asked if marriage were really as bad as all that. Again, a solecism, but recitation of one's own work in public appears to make such a primitive response appear legitimate. There I stood, after all. I'd survived, a perfectly ordinary woman in a nice suit.

So there's this conflict within marriage for a woman poet (it exists for men too, but men appear to be covered by the convention of the romantic poet who isn't a household item in the first place, and who, in the second, glides from one inspiring woman to the next). Writing about the conflict, I put in jeopardy what I have been at great pains to preserve, and for this reason, I suspect: that literature itself is about fidelity and the efforts to escape it, with all the accompanying pains and joys. So have I managed to maneuver myself into this difficult position on purpose? And to venture one step further: can it be that writing poetry is not worth it? Look at the amount of bad poetry being written: who can justify that? And yet most good poets have been bad poets once. Can anyone, least of all a woman responsible for children, afford to write badly while mastery is gained, considering the pains and the amount of time poetry demands?

Well, yes. It's easy to come down on the side of the angels, but I think it's worth saying that the effort to write a decent poem and to move people with it is an engagement with the truth, which shapes your life and, with luck, the lives of others. And more than that: when a poem appears to work, even in my intolerably rough and ready approximations, there's a sublime moment in which all comes together and sheds light.

Illinois Poetry Series
Laurence Lieberman, Editor

Healing Song for the Inner Ear
Michael S. Harper (1984)

The Passion of the Right-Angled Man
T. R. Hummer (1984)

Dear John, Dear Coltrane
Michael S. Harper (1985)

Poems from the Sangamon
John Knoepfle (1985)

In It
Stephen Berg (1986)

The Ghosts of Who We Were
Phyllis Thompson (1986)

Moon in a Mason Jar
Robert Wrigley (1986)

Lower-Class Heresy
T. R. Hummer (1987)

Poems: New and Selected
Frederick Morgan (1987)

Furnace Harbor: A Rhapsody of the
    North Country
Philip D. Church (1988)

Bad Girl, with Hawk
Nance Van Winckel (1988)

Blue Tango
Michael Van Walleghen (1989)

Eden
Dennis Schmitz (1989)

Waiting for Poppa at the Smithtown
    Diner
Peter Serchuk (1990)

Great Blue
Brendan Galvin (1990)

What My Father Believed
Robert Wrigley (1991)

Something Grazes Our Hair
S. J. Marks (1991)

Walking the Blind Dog
G. E. Murray (1992)

The Sawdust War
Jim Barnes (1992)

The God of Indeterminacy
Sandra McPherson (1993)

Off-Season at the Edge of the World
Debora Greger (1994)

Counting the Black Angels
Len Roberts (1994)

Oblivion
Stephen Berg (1995)

To Us, All Flowers Are Roses
Lorna Goodison (1995)

Honorable Amendments
Michael S. Harper (1995)

Points of Departure
Miller Williams (1995)

Dance Script with Electric Ballerina
Alice Fulton (reissue, 1996)

To the Bone: New and Selected Poems
Sydney Lea (1996)

Floating on Solitude
Dave Smith (3–vol. reissue, 1996)

Bruised Paradise
Kevin Stein (1996)

Walt Whitman Bathing
David Wagoner (1996)

Rough Cut
Thomas Swiss (1997)

Paris
Jim Barnes (1997)

The Ways We Touch
Miller Williams (1997)

The Rooster Mask
Henry Hart (1998)

The Trouble-Making Finch
Len Roberts (1998)

Grazing
Ira Sadoff (1998)

Turn Thanks
Lorna Goodison (1999)

Traveling Light: Collected and New
Poems
David Wagoner (1999)

Some Jazz a While: Collected Poems
Miller Williams (1999)

The Iron City
John Bensko (2000)

Songlines in Michaeltree: New and
Collected Poems
Michael S. Harper (2000)

Pursuit of a Wound
Sydney Lea (2000)

The Pebble: Old and New Poems
Mairi MacInnes (2000)

National Poetry Series

Eroding Witness
Nathaniel Mackey (1985)
Selected by Michael S. Harper

Palladium
Alice Fulton (1986)
Selected by Mark Strand

Cities in Motion
Sylvia Moss (1987)
Selected by Derek Walcott

The Hand of God and a Few Bright
Flowers
William Olsen (1988)
Selected by David Wagoner

The Great Bird of Love
Paul Zimmer (1989)
Selected by William Stafford

Stubborn
Roland Flint (1990)
Selected by Dave Smith

The Surface
Laura Mullen (1991)
Selected by C. K. Williams

The Dig
Lynn Emanuel (1992)
Selected by Gerald Stern

My Alexandria
Mark Doty (1993)
Selected by Philip Levine

The High Road to Taos
Martin Edmunds (1994)
Selected by Donald Hall

Theater of Animals
Samn Stockwell (1995)
Selected by Louise Glück

The Broken World
Marcus Cafagña (1996)
Selected by Yusef Komunyakaa

Nine Skies
A. V. Christie (1997)
Selected by Sandra McPherson

Lost Wax
Heather Ramsdell (1998)
Selected by James Tate

So Often the Pitcher Goes to Water
until It Breaks
Rigoberto González (1999)
Selected by Ai

Other Poetry Volumes

Local Men and *Domains*
James Whitehead (1987)

Her Soul beneath the Bone: Women's
Poetry on Breast Cancer
Edited by Leatrice Lifshitz (1988)

Days from a Dream Almanac
Dennis Tedlock (1990)

Working Classics: Poems on
Industrial Life
*Edited by Peter Oresick and Nicholas
Coles* (1990)

Hummers, Knucklers, and Slow
Curves: Contemporary Baseball
Poems
Edited by Don Johnson (1991)

The Double Reckoning of Christo-
pher Columbus
Barbara Helfgott Hyett (1992)

Selected Poems
Jean Garrigue (1992)

New and Selected Poems, 1962–92
Laurence Lieberman (1993)

The Dig and *Hotel Fiesta*
Lynn Emanuel (1994)

For a Living: The Poetry of Work
*Edited by Nicholas Coles and Peter
Oresick* (1995)

The Tracks We Leave: Poems on
Endangered Wildlife of North
America
Barbara Helfgott Hyett (1996)

Peasants Wake for Fellini's *Casanova*
and Other Poems
*Andrea Zanzotto; edited and translated
by John P. Welle and Ruth Feldman;
drawings by Federico Fellini and Au-
gusto Murer* (1997)

Moon in a Mason Jar and *What My
Father Believed*
Robert Wrigley (1997)

The Wild Card: Selected Poems,
Early and Late
*Karl Shapiro; edited by Stanley Kunitz
and David Ignatow* (1998)

Turtle, Swan and *Bethlehem in Broad
Daylight*
Mark Doty (2000)

Typeset in 9.5/14 ITC Stone Serif
with Cezanne display
Designed by Paula Newcomb
Composed by Jim Proefrock
at the University of Illinois Press
Manufactured by Cushing-Malloy, Inc.

University of Illinois Press
1325 South Oak Street
Champaign, IL 61820–6903
www.press.uillinois.edu

10/12/2000

DATE DUE   J

WITHDRAWN